The United States Acquires
The Philippines:
Consensus vs. Reality

THE CREDIBILITY OF INSTITUTIONS, POLICIES AND LEADERSHIP
A Series funded by the Hewlett Foundation
Kenneth W. Thompson, *Series Editor*

The United States Acquires The Philippines: Consensus vs. Reality

The Credibility of Institutions, Policies and Leadership
Volume 15

Louis J. Halle

With a Preface by Kenneth W. Thompson

University Press of America
Lanham • New York • London

Copyright © 1985 by

University Press of America,® Inc.

4720 Boston Way
Lanham, MD 20706

3 Henrietta Street
London WC2E 8LU England

Co-published by arrangement with
The White Burkett Miller Center of Public Affairs,
The University of Virginia

Library of Congress Cataloging in Publication Data

Halle, Louis Joseph, 1910-
  The United States acquires the Philippines.

  (The Credibility of institutions, policies, and
leadership ; v. 15)
  Includes bibliographical references.
    1. United States—Foreign relations—Philippines.
2. Philippines—Foreign relations—United States.
3. Philippines—History—1898-1946. 4. United States—
Foreign relations—War of 1898. I. Title. II. Series.
E183.8.P6H35   1985   327.730599   85-9233
ISBN 0-8191-4759-1 (alk. paper)
ISBN 0-8191-4760-5 (pbk. : alk. paper)

to Urs Schwarz,
journalist and historian,
colleague,
and all-weather friend

Contents

Preface

In its original and unpublished form, Louis J. Halle's study in the making of American foreign policy was awarded the Phi Beta Kappa Prize at the University of Virginia. Some of it was later summarized, rather drastically, in his *Dream and Reality: Aspects of American Foreign Policy*. It constitutes the core of the book that follows.

After having for many years been directly involved in the making of American foreign policy in Washington, Halle became a Research Professor in the Woodrow Wilson Department of Foreign Affairs at the University of Virginia. He later became professor at the Graduate Institute of International Studies in Geneva, Switzerland, a standpoint from which he has been able to cultivate the perspective on American foreign policy represented by *The Cold War as History* and other books on international politics.

Although he has now acquired Swiss nationality, the pages that follow were written from the position of an American whose mind was shaped by the poignant experience of grappling, inside the Office of the Secretary of State, with the dilemmas that the American policymaker has to resolve.

Kenneth W. Thompson

Consensus vs. Reality

Introduction

Men and nations are governed in their actions by ideas of propriety that, in the process of historical evolution, are subject to constant change or replacement.[1] It follows that the historian can rightly understand their actions only in terms of the particular ideas of propriety that prevailed at the moment when those actions were undertaken. He must have the faculty of reexperiencing in his own imagination the full validity that such ideas had for the actors of another time and place. This requires the capacity to liberate himself from the ideas that seem eternally valid from the momentary standpoint of his own time and place. If, for example, he lives in an anti-imperialistic age, he may feel a moral revulsion against the idea that the civilized white man does well to impose his civilization on the heathen; but he will fail to understand British and American imperialism at the turn of the century if he regards it as simply a flouting of the anti-imperialism that constitutes the propriety of his own time. The imperialist of 1900 may be as moral as the anti-imperialist of our time, but in terms of a different morality. The historian of our time, although he prefers his own morality, has to recognize that the prevailing morality of 1900 seemed as valid to those who were living then.

The ideas of propriety that prevail in any particular society at any particular time determine its consensus, if any, on such issues of national policy as arise. At the end of the 1890s, however, two opposed ideas, each with its powerful following in the American society, prevented the establishment of a nation-wide consensus. One was the

---

1. This is a principal theme of my *Men and Nations*, Princeton 1962, 1965.

anti-imperalistic idea, its roots going back to the revolt against British imperialism that culminated in the American Declaration of Independence. The other was that of great-power paternalism, implying the obligation of the mature and civilized powers to keep order among the smaller and less civilized societies.[2]

The United States "liberated" the Philippines from Spain in 1898 without having intended to do so, and therefore without having given any thought to what their status should be after that had happened. When the accomplished fact raised the unanticipated question, there was no consensus on how to answer it because the nation remained divided between the two mutually opposed ideas that then became the subject of bitter national debate.

Consensus, however, is not the only factor that determines national policy. A more important factor—one that is, indeed, intractable—is that of strategic circumstances. While the debate between the two opposed ideas, imperialism and anti-imperialism, was conducted at a high level of abstraction, ineluctable strategic circumstances assumed command, resolving the issue as it applied to the Philippines. These circumstances, which had been anticipated by neither side in the debate, defeated even the imperialists, who saw too late the disastrous strategic implications of their imperialism.

No doubt there is a lesson here. The application of the normative ideas to which we give our allegiance should take account of strategic reality—which is to say that any national consensus on policy should take account of it.

●　　●　　●

The sequence of events that left a troubled American nation in possession of the Philippines is related here from the viewpoint of one who thinks in terms of how foreign policy is usually made and how it might better be made. The dominant impression that it leaves is of lack of choice. Decisions did not make circumstances so much as circumstances made decisions. This, I venture to say, matches the experience of every statesman who finds himself nominally invested with the power of government and expected to use it in order to command events. "I

---

2. For a revelatory study of these opposed concepts, in their historical evolution, see *Sovereign Equality among States: the History of an Idea* by Robert A. Klein, Toronto, 1974. This book should be famous.

claim not to have controlled events," Abraham Lincoln wrote a year before his death, "but confess plainly that events have controlled me."[3] No one who achieves political power finds himself free to do much of what he had intended to do when he had anticipated its achievement. Once achieved, all sorts of strategic circumstances limit his freedom. This applies to the leaders of authoritarian regimes as well as to those who are hedged about with constitutional restrictions. A strong and able leader will manage to do just a little more than one who is weak and inept, but he will still find himself more limited in his possibilities than those who do not have his experience can well understand.

The victory of circumstances over men with aspirations that are essentially noble is the basis of tragedy, whether personal tragedy or the tragedy of history. The circumstances, however, are not all external to us humans and beyond reach of our remedies. When we look for those that bear most immediately on the course of history we find that many are related to ignorance, to misconception, and to human immoderation in various forms; and we find that they are associated with those ideas of propriety on which the consensus of any particular time and place is based. Being what the American nation was in 1898, its acquisition of an unfortunate responsibility for the Philippines appears to have been inevitable; but surely it would not have been inevitable if it had been a nation of Talleyrands and Bismarcks.

Let us, then, learn from experience.

---

3. Letter to A. G. Hodges of 4 April 1864.

CHAPTER I

Destiny and the Philippines

> Outlying colonies, inadequately defended, are, in time of war, sources of serious weakness to the mother country. This military axiom was never better exemplified than in the case of Spain at the time of her struggle with the United States.
> —*John D. Long, Secretary of the Navy, 1897 to 1902*

Two days before the formal conclusion of the Spanish-American War, on February 4, 1899, the United States found itself engaged in another war. Our American soldiers, seven thousand miles from home, had come to blows with Filipinos who were resisting our attempt to subjugate their country. The new war was to last several times as long as the old and to cost more in blood and treasure alike. It was to be characterized by a reciprocal brutality that could be matched in the history of the times only by the atrocities which had marked the recent struggle of the Cubans to achieve their independence of Spain.

We had become engaged in the Philippine War without considered intention and we remained in it without any clear purpose beyond the military pacification of the islands. Our own American history made it easy for us to understand what the Filipinos were fighting for. But what were we fighting for? What was the American policy that justified this military adventure on the shores of Asia? How was it that we found ourselves trying to conquer a land which, as was widely apparent, we would have done well to refuse as a gift?

The fact is that we could not know what our purpose was because we did not know how we came to be acting as we were. Our position was that of a man in a dream who finds himself doing what he never meant to do, saying what he never meant to say. Even our "expansionists" were hard put for arguments to support our action in terms of justifiable intention or national interest. Theodore Roosevelt, who had promoted the original attack on the Philippines, said that we had been "forced by the exigencies of war" to take them.[1]

Plutarch tells how Julius Caesar hesitated, pondering the consequences, before he embarked on his irrevocable passage of the Rubicon. In the case of that commitment to power politics in the Far East which the acquisition of the Philippines meant for us, our pondering took place after we had already made the crossing.

When we went to war with Spain on April 25, 1898, virtually no one in the United States had any notion of acquiring an Asiatic empire. It was an exceptional American who knew where the Philippine Islands were, or, perhaps, had even heard of them. Those whom we identify today with their acquisition appear to have had no thought, as yet, of acquiring them. Apparently it was not in the mind of Theodore Roosevelt, then Assistant Secretary of the Navy, when he made the arrangements for Commodore Dewey's attack on the Spanish squadron at Manila[2]; it had not occurred to the Commodore[3]; and Captain Mahan, the philosopher of expansionism, experienced misgivings when it first appeared that we might be committed to their acquisition.[4] Mahan, who had conspired with Roosevelt and Senator Lodge for an aggressive naval policy in the Pacific, later wrote that the vision of the expansionists themselves, up to the war with Spain, "reached not past Hawaii, which also, as touching the United States, they regarded from the point of view of defense rather than as a stepping-stone to any farther influence in the world."[5]

Not only did we have no thought of acquiring the Philippines before we entered upon the course of action by which they became ours, their acquisition, if it had been proposed, would have been regarded as repugnant to our national policy. We believed that a nation like ours,

---

1. Message to 1st Session, 57th Congress.
2. S. F. Bemis, *The United States as a World Power,* New York: Holt, 1950, p. 6. Also, further discussion in this and the following two chapters.
3. George Dewey, *Autobiography,* New York, 1913, p. 185.
4. Mahan to H. C. Lodge, 7/27/98; cited by Livesey, *Mahan on Sea Power,* Oklahoma, 1947, pp. 181–187.
5. A. T. Mahan, *The Problem of Asia,* Boston, 1905, pp. 7–8.

dedicated to representative government with the consent of the governed, could not include within its jurisdiction some seven million
distant subjects, unqualified for citizenship, over which it exercised the
kind of colonial rule against which it had declared its own independence.
Many Americans questioned whether our Constitution, with its guar-
antees of human rights, would allow it. Even if these bars had not
existed, our people had shown before, as they have since, their aversion
for the kind of empire which the European great powers had been
establishing among the world's pariahs. The burden of administering a
dependency like the Philippines might well be expected to outweigh
any advantages to be gained by its exploitation. Our policy was clearly
against it.

This was certainly the judgment of the nation before our people
received the surprising news that our flag was, in fact, flying over the
islands. A decade later it would have been hard to find any responsible
opinion, including that of Roosevelt and of Mahan, to dissent wholly
from the view that our acquisition of responsibility for them was unfortunate. Yet the fact remains that, early in 1899, we found ourselves
already committed to the prosecution of a long and painful war for their
subjugation.

The paradox of 1898 is that, in this year, our course of action on
the international scene began to diverge from our national policy. This
happened because, as everyone recognized at the time, we were not
ourselves determining that course of action. It was being determined
for us by what we sometimes called "circumstances," sometimes
"destiny."

How could this be?

The question is interesting from several points of view. It bears on
the argument between freedom and predestination, on the limits within
which nations may exercise choice in making their own history, on the
meaning of political morality, on the pressures to which governments
must submit, on differences between democratic and autocratic rule,
on the problem of leadership, on the nature of foreign policy. However,
in the light of our historic experience since 1898 it has an immediate
practical significance. For in the half century that followed we were not
able to escape from the course of events inaugurated by "the Great
Aberration of 1898." We were repeatedly moved by "circumstances"
or by "destiny" more than by any policy of our own, and therefore we
were not able to "make" policy. More than once we repeated our
unthinking behavior of 1898, crossing other Rubicons under the dic-
tation of "circumstances" without knowing that we were doing so until

we were already over. In the best part of a century after Dewey's famous victory at Manila Bay, our country poured out blood and treasure in the Far East for purposes which it could not confidently justify or did not itself understand. It appears to have been drawn by fugitive expediency into increasingly perilous courses without warrant in reason, justice, or the national interest. It repeatedly met the problems of a momentary present in ways that, as we now see, made for the accumulation of troubles in the long future. To overcome passing emergencies it assumed large commitments from which, when the emergencies had passed, it could not extricate itself. At the same time, in the absence of any convincing cause our people were unwilling to pay the price in militarization and diplomatic concession required for the support of these commitments. The consequent insolvency of our position in the Far East finally produced, in succession, the Japanese attack on Pearl Harbor, the unrewarding struggle with China in the 1950s, and our final defeat in Vietnam.

The divergence between our action and our policy, which began in 1898, was reflected at home by a split in our body politic. For two generations we were at war with ourselves over what our role in the Far East should be. The issue of aggressive self-assertion or self-restraint in the Far East, which was the subject of our great debate in 1900, was still subject of our great debate in 1950, and still in the 1970s. This inner conflict, persisting so long and rooted so deeply, had increasingly unhappy consequences. It was the cause of our inability to make policy. Together with the increasing burdens and dangers of our position in the Far East, and our frustration, it shook our confidence in ourselves and our leadership, culminating in manifestations of mass demoralization, represented most notably by McCarthyism. In the 1950s we at last provided the rest of the world with the spectacle of half our nation accusing the other half of treason.

The picture sketched so briefly above is simplified. It omits much. Nevertheless, a pattern of repeated behavior seems to mark our involvement in the Far East since 1898, unfolding in an accumulation of dangers and difficulties. The existence of our inner trouble, whatever its nature, is clear. If we are to go to its root we should begin with an inquiry into the nature of the "circumstances" or the "destiny" that caused us to gain possession of the Philippines as we did, by our own action although against our will.

● ● ●

The Spanish-American War was not made by statesmen acting with deliberation, weighing their responsibilities, and taking the requirements of national policy as their guide. In 1898 our nation had, for the moment, lost its sobriety and abandoned itself to glory. This was a people's war into which our government was swept by public opinion.

What does it mean to say this? Who were the people? What was public opinion?

Public opinion, as far as governments are concerned, is not the spontaneous expression of the population as a statistical total. It is, rather, the opinion expressed by those who can influence significant parts of the population to a degree which might be politically decisive. In 1898 this meant, most notably, newpaper publishers. The yellow press, competing in sensationalism, deliberately embarked on a campaign against Spanish treatment of the Cubans as a means of increasing its circulation. It elaborated atrocity stories to arouse alike the animal passion and the self-righteousness of its public. The reader who was secretly stirred by accounts of Spanish soldiers mistreating Cuban girls salved his conscience with the sense of virtuous indignation that accompanied their telling. The worse his private shame, perhaps, the greater the compensating ardour with which he was moved to advocate in public a policy of righteous war.

We touch, here, one cause of the popular pressure for war against Spain. There were others; and underlying them all a passing phase of national psychology that one would hesitate to explore, if only because of the scope and obscurity of its ramifications.[6] The point is that public pressures were developed, emotional pressures of a nature hard for any government to deal with; since to those who do not share their sobriety the reasons of the sober sound like the counsels of cowardice.

In terms of cold reason the case for a war against Spain was poor. Spain had not violated any engagement with the United States or dishonored any undertaking to which the United States was a party. It had done no significant injury to our country, nothing to constitute a legitimate *casus belli*. It was merely trying to hold its own in one of its possessions under circumstances with which we would ourselves become

---

6. This much may be noted. Around the turn of the century the two new arrivals as powers on the world scene, the United States and Germany, were moved by the newness of their arrival to behave, internationally, with a combination of touchiness and arrogance which the former outgrew.

familiar sooner than we would have thought possible. If the yellow press had not flaunted the issue of Spanish oppression our country would surely not have concerned itself as it did.

At the same time, we could not have been unconcerned. Humanitarian appeals gain by propinquity. The suffering of a next-door neighbor necessarily moves us as suffering at a distance does not. Moreover, our expansion to the west coast of our continent, involving us in a two-ocean defense, now made the Caribbean Sea in which Cuba lay an area of vital, strategic significance for us. While these considerations gave us no jurisdiction over what went on in Cuba, we could hardly be expected not to show an interest, and the interest we showed was bound to be partisan.

Spain's inherited position in Cuba and Puerto Rico, a last remnant of her empire in the New World, had become obsolete and increasingly untenable by the end of the nineteenth century. It would have to be adjusted. But the Spanish government recognized this and there was no reason to doubt that, given time, patience, and the absence of public excitement in either country, the adjustment could be accomplished without war. It had, in fact, almost been accomplished before the war broke out. The Spanish government, moving as fast as an impassioned public opinion in its own country allowed, was cooperating earnestly with our government to achieve a diplomatic solution. Twenty days before we actually went to war, our essential demands had already been met.

By this time, however, the yellow press had another case for incitement to war. An explosion had sunk the U.S.S. *Maine* in Havana harbor. The suggestion that it had been sunk by the agency of the Spanish Government remains implausible in the absence of evidence and in the light of that government's efforts to avoid provocation. This incident, however, finally enabled the yellow press to get the war which it wanted and for which it was more than willing to take responsibility before history. The honor of our country was invoked to avenge the sinking of the *Maine*.

The Administration of President McKinley bowed, at last, to a basic rule of politics: where you cannot lead you had better follow. It had tried, like its predecessor, to calm public opinion and to achieve a diplomatic settlement with Spain before too late. Now it saw an excited Congress, moved by the mass emotion, preparing to act on its own to have a war. It fell into step and, two days after the Spanish capitulation to our demands, the President sent his war message to Congress. The yellow press was able to boast of the war which it, rather than a responsible government, had made.

●   ●   ●

Historians and statesmen since Thucydides have recognized, as a prime danger inherent in war, that states which embark on it tend to lose control of their own destiny. Unforeseen circumstances, emerging as the fighting proceeds, impose themselves on national policy. Passions are aroused that cannot be governed by reason, ethics, or self-interest. Moderation comes to be regarded as cowardice. Governments buffeted in the storms of fear, anger, and exultation cannot keep to courses set before the storms broke. This is true particularly for states in which the people as a whole are involved either because they must be disposed to pay the price of victory or because the government depends on their suffrage.

A typical manifestation of this danger is the repeated inability of states to keep to the limited objectives for which they have gone to war, once victory comes within their reach. Our war with Spain may have been unnecessary, but there was no doubt of the precise and limited objective for which we entered upon it. It was to liberate the island of Cuba. This objective was made explicit in the joint resolution passed by Congress on April 19, 1898, which further disclaimed territorial greed by foreswearing any disposition to acquire Cuba for ourselves.

The Spanish war presented no grave military problem for us. One of the reasons why Spain's position in Cuba had become obsolete was that her naval power had diminished to the point where it could no longer defend the island or support the Spanish troops on it in case of war. There was, as it transpired, no military need to attack Spain elsewhere. We did not, for example have to campaign against the Balearic Islands in the Mediterranean. Local wars have often been limited in this fashion. Among the practicable alternatives open to us as a nation, that of confining the war to the vicinity of Cuba was certainly one. From one point of view it seems the obvious thing to have done.

There is another point of view, however, that has represented military orthodoxy since the days of Clausewitz. According to it, the prime military objective in warfare is not the capture of territory but the destruction of the enemy's power and will to fight. Admiral Dewey was not making a statement that was likely to give anyone pause when he said in his memoirs: "While we remained at war with Spain our purpose must be to strike at the power of Spain wherever possible."[7] Military men, then as now, were brought up to accept this concept as basic. Our own people did not question it in connection with any of the three wars that we fought between 1898 and 1945, although it subsequently became an issue of the Korean War.

Because this concept was taken for granted, no special act of decision was needed to include the Philippines within the scope of our military operations. It would, rather, have taken a special act of decision to exclude them. In the absence of such an act, plans and preparations for a Philippine campaign were made at a subordinate level and as a matter of routine. Strained relations with Spain under the Cleveland Administration had already prompted Cleveland's Secretary of the Navy to maintain a naval squadron in the western Pacific, where the Spaniards also maintained a squadron.[8] Dewey's predecessor as commander of that squadron had, apparently on his own initiative, made plans for an attack on the Spanish forces in the Philippines. He turned these plans over to Dewey with his command.[9] The new Assistant Secretary, Roosevelt, was not being original when he included operations against the Philippines in the action that he recommended to the Secretary of the Navy for the contingency of a war with Spain.

It is true that Secretary Long was uneasy at Roosevelt's general boldness; but he apparently thought of no reason for taking issue with the plan itself. When, ten days after the sinking of the *Maine*, he gave himself an afternoon off, Roosevelt took the occasion to dispatch a cablegram to Dewey, instructing him that, in the event of war, his duty would be "to see that the Spanish squadron does not leave the Asiatic coast, and then offensive operations in Philippines."[10] Upon returning to the Department, Long sent his subordinate a gentle reprimand in the form of a memorandum, saying: "Do not take any such step affecting the policy of the Administration without consulting the President or me. I am not away from town, and my intention was to have you look after the routine of the office while I got a quiet day off." But he did not take issue with the substance of the instruction to Dewey, adding rather: "I write to you because I am anxious to have no occasion for a sensation

---

7. George Dewey, *Autobiography, op. cit.*, p. 239.

8. John D. Long, *The New American Navy*, New York, 1903, I, p. 168.

9. *Ibid*, p. 179.

10. *Appendix to the Report of the Chief of the Bureau of Navigation, Navy Department, 1898*, Washington, 1898, p. 65.

in the papers."[11] Like the President, he was letting such policy as is implicit in war-plans be made by default. At least, he was accepting the war-plans made by his Department without question, if also without enthusiasm. The conduct of war was not a subject with which either he or the President was familiar.

When war had in effect begun, on April 21, with the blockade of Cuba, Long conveyed to the President "the unanimous opinion of the Department . . . that we should strike at once at the Spanish fleet in the Philippines." The President, according to Long, "thought it not quite time." On the 24th, however, a cable from Dewey reported that, in response to the request of the Governor of Hong Kong, based on England's declaration of neutrality, his squadron was leaving for nearby Mirs Bay, where he would await instructions. At a meeting in the White House, an order to Dewey was drafted and the President approved it.[12] It read: "War has commenced. . . . Proceed at once to Philippine Islands. Commence operations particularly against the Spanish fleet. You must capture vessels or destroy. Use utmost endeavor."[13] No one, apparently, thought of this order in terms of the significance it might have for the general position of the United States in the Far East. It represented merely the implementation of a war strategy that had never been questioned.[14]

---

11. Quoted by Walter Millis in *The Martial Spirit*, Boston, 1931, p. 112.
12. A controversy later arose over the circumstances in which the order was prepared. See letter from A. S. Crowninshield to Long, July 3, 1901, *Papers of John Davis Long*, Massachusetts Historical Society Collections, Vol. 78, 1939, p. 379; and Long, *The New American Navy, op. cit.*, I, pp. 181–182.
13. *Appendix to the Report of the Chief of the Bureau of Navigation, op. cit.*, p. 67.
14. Rear Admiral F. E. Chadwick (in *The Relations of the United States and Spain: The Spanish-American War*, New York, 1911, 2 vols., Vol. I, p. 39) writes: "Had the conquest and retention of the Philippines been in the mind of the American government the two powerful monitors *Monterey* and *Monadnock* should at once have been added [to Dewey's squadron], instead of delaying the departure from California of the former until June 11, and of the latter until June 23. That they were not sent at once is but added proof that the holding of the islands was an after-thought." This view has further corroboration in the fact that no plans or preparations were made until after Dewey's victory to provide troops for the taking even of

Dewey carried out his mission with punctilio and daring. He proceeded from Hong Kong to the Bay of Manila, where the Spanish squadron lay, and destroyed it at its anchorage without the loss of a single American life.

All this was done in the public view, so to speak, while the world held its breath. Dewey's departure from Hong Kong and his destination were front-page news on April 25. For the next week the world speculated about the coming encounter. On April 26, a *New York Times* editorial referred to the "strange probability that the first engagement of a conflict which pertains to the possession of an island off the eastern coast of North America may be fought in the waters of a group of islands off the eastern coast of Asia, half the world away from the origin of the war."

The American people had been showing increasing frustration at the lack of any heroic military action coincident with the outbreak of war, and the government in Washington had been coming under mounting criticism for timidity. For five days after it left the Asiatic coast, nothing was heard of Dewey's squadron. Then, on May 2, the news of the victory came—not from Dewey, who was not heard from until May 7 (since he had no direct cable facilities), but by way of Madrid. The relief and rejoicing were universal, but no place more so, one suspects, than in the corridors of Washington where the public pressure for action had been so keenly felt. A *Times* dispatch of May 2 from that city reported: " . . . this has been a day of rejoicing and congratulations for the Administration. . . ." It added: "The victory has scarcely been fully reported before the fact flashes upon the Administration, as it has upon the European diplomatic circles, that the United States Government has suddenly acquired a status in the East that was not at all looked for, and that may greatly change the discussion of Eastern problems."

This is not the last time that we shall have occasion to note how implications of an event that become obvious immediately after it takes place remain unforeseen throughout the period in which it is anticipated only.

●   ●   ●

Manila; and in the failure even to consider the acquisition of Spain's Ladrone and Caroline Islands (not just Guam) to protect our communications with the Philippines.

The Philippine strategy was developed as a matter internal to the Navy Department rather than by our Government as a whole. There is nothing to show, for example, that the State Department interested itself. Even the War Department appears to have been unconcerned with it. Consequently, when the Spanish squadron had been destroyed, Dewey found himself without those landing forces which he would need to carry out the "offensive operations in Philippines" that he had been instructed to undertake after dealing with the squadron. This omission also became obvious to Washington in the moment of victory, and not until then.

Although Dewey himself was not heard from until May 7, on May 3 the Commanding General of the Army recommended to the Secretary of War that General Thomas M. Anderson be sent "to occupy the Philippine Islands," in command of certain specified troops; and on May 4 the President ordered that these troops be assembled at San Francisco.[15] This represented the decision, made without forethought, to take the Philippines, whether temporarily or permanently.

The energy now manifested by the Army was impressive, as if in the atmosphere of public exultation it felt impelled to make up for time lost while the Navy had been alert and active. It had few regular troops to spare for the Philippines, but it immediately undertook the organization, around regular units as cadres, of large volunteer formations. When, in response to an inquiry from Washington, Dewey reported on May 15 that he would need five thousand men, plans were already well under way that resulted in sending out four times that number.

But here, again, action was ahead of policy and thought. Major General Wesley Merritt, the officer selected to command the Philippine expedition, was not clear on what his mission was. Having had an interview with the President on May 12, he wrote him on the 15th: "I do not yet know whether it is your desire to subdue and hold all of the Spanish territory in the islands, or merely to seize and hold the capital."[16] A few days later he was objecting that an estimate of 15,425 troops by General Miles, Commanding General of the Army, was inadequate "when the work to be done consists of conquering a territory 7,000 miles from our base . . . inhabited by 14,000,000 [sic] of people, the

---

15. Adjutant General's Office, *Correspondence relating to the War with Spain . . .*", Washington, 1902, 2 vols., II, p. 635.
16. *Ibid,* II, pp. 645–646.

majority of whom will regard us with the intense hatred born of race and religion."

To this General Miles replied: "The force ordered at this time is not expected to carry on a war to conquer an extensive territory, and the chief object . . . was to suggest a means of quickly establishing a strong garrison to command the harbor of Manila and to relieve the United States fleet under Admiral Dewey with the least possible delay."[17]

One cannot escape the impression that here, as throughout this history, President McKinley did not put himself in command of events. Perhaps this was because, like everyone else at the time, he was confused by their nearness and speed, and could not see their meaning.

In a letter of May 19 to the Secretary of War, the President finally defined the mission of the expeditionary force in terms of what had been rendered necessary by events. He wrote that:

> The destruction of the Spanish fleet at Manila, followed
> by the taking of the naval station at Cavite, the paroling
> of the garrisons, and acquisition of the control of the bay,
> have rendered it necessary, in the further prosecution of
> the measures adopted by this Government for the purpose
> of bringing about an honorable and durable peace with
> Spain, to send an army of occupation to the Philippines
> for the two-fold purpose of completing the reduction of
> the Spanish power in that quarter and of giving order and
> security to the islands while in the possession of the
> United States. . . .
>
> The first effect of the military occupation of the enemy's
> territory is the severance of the former political relations
> of the inhabitants and the establishment of a new political
> power. . . ."[18]

Without looking forward as far as the post-war future, but merely trying to stay abreast of the present, our Government had concluded that events "rendered it necessary" to take possession of the Philippine Islands.

●   ●   ●

---

17. *Ibid*, II, pp. 647–649.
18. *Ibid*, II, pp. 676–678.

When the Spanish-American War came, Congress and the country had been debating a proposal to annex the Hawaiian Islands, which might otherwise fall to Japan or a European power that, basing its navy upon them, would be in a position to threaten our west coast. Although the Polynesian natives had by then sunk to a minority and American interests already occupied a commanding position in the Islands, the proposal seemed unlikely to overcome the opposition of those who believed that a country like ours was morally and constitutionally precluded from acquiring any overseas empire with a foreign population.

Under the circumstances, the notion that we might not be in a position to relinquish the Philippines when the war was over was too novel for immediate apprehension in the crowded days after Dewey's victory. It took time to sink in. To some it seemed, at first, that we should naturally hold them as collateral for a Spanish indemnity at the war's end, returning them to Spain upon its payment.[19] To others it seemed logical that we should grant them their independence, as we intended to do with Cuba. Various newspapers rather assumed that, with the war ended, we would turn them over to one of the other European powers, preferably Great Britain if she would have them.

Commenting editorially on May 3, the *New York Times* found it unthinkable that we would ever return the islands to Spain. Exploring alternatives, it added that "nobody pretends that the natives of the Philippines are fit for self-government, as we believe the Cubans to be. On the other hand, all the arguments against the annexation of Hawaii are available with even greater force, against our retention of the Philippines for ourselves." It concluded that we had already incurred a responsibility in seizing them which could be discharged only by having Great Britain take them off our hands, "leaving us only a naval station in them."

The following day the *Times,* in one and the same editorial, was saying that "we could not in any event take the islands for ourselves," and also that if Britain "declines to take them on reasonable terms we must even retain them for ourselves," since we could neither return them to Spain "nor yet hand them over to their negroid aborigines and Malay inhabitants." It was thus foreseeing the possibility of a dilemma in which every possible alternative was impossible to contemplate— such a dilemma as is not unique in the conduct of foreign affairs.

---

19. As late as June 5, the peace terms which the President had in mind included return of the Philippines. See Tyler Dennett, *John Hay: from Poetry to Politics,* New York, 1934, p. 190.

Finally, by May 9, the *Times* had at last brought itself to contemplate what could not be contemplated at first. It saw that we could not transfer the islands "to any European or Asiatic power without stirring up strifes and jealousies that would endanger our friendly relations with other powers, and in the unstable condition of Eastern affairs might precipitate a war. . . ." By elimination of alternatives, only one remained. "It is becoming plainer every day," it concluded "that paramount necessity will compel us to assume for a time of which we cannot now see the end the duty of governing and controlling the Philippine Islands." (Here was the unforeseen consequence of the unnecessary decision to attack them in the first place.)

Even Theodore Roosevelt, who had been a prime mover in our assault on the Philippines and who had contemplated the action at least since the previous September, appears not to have made up his mind so quickly. On May 25 he wrote to his fellow conspirator, Senator Lodge, expressing the earnest hope "that no truce will be granted and that peace will only be made on consideration of Cuba being independent, Porto Rico ours, and the Philippines taken away from Spain."[20] It was only later that he came out for annexation.

The President, too, was still behind the march of events, trying to catch up with them. Being at a loss to know what we should do with the Philippines, now that they were at our disposal, he postponed decision. One of the conditions that he made for a truce with Spain, on July 30, was that we should continue to occupy "the city, bay and harbor of Manila pending the conclusion of a treaty of peace which shall determine the control, disposition, and the government of the Philippines."[21]

At first his thought was to demand of Spain the cession of Luzon only, the other islands to be returned to her. With the passage of time, however, he came to the conclusion that we must take the whole archipelago.

In his instructions of September 16 to the American commissioners appointed to negotiate the peace with Spain, the President wrote:

> Without any original thought of complete or even partial
> acquisition, the presence and success of our arms at

20. *Selections from the Correspondence of Theodore Roosevelt and Henry Cabot Lodge,* New York, 1925, Vol. I, p. 301.
21. Quoted by Dennett, *Americans in Eastern Asia,* p. 620.

Manila imposes upon us obligations which we cannot
disregard. The march of events rules and overrules human
action. . . . We cannot be unmindful that without any
desire or design on our part the war has brought us new
duties and responsibilities which we must meet and
discharge as becomes a great nation on whose growth and
career from the beginning the Ruler of Nations has
plainly written the high command and pledge of
civilization.[22]

We may not doubt that the President, who sought divine guidance
for his decision on the Philippines, wrote this with sincerity. But it
confronts us with a paradox that goes to the root of our present inquiry.
It virtually states, in its first two sentences, that "the presence and
success of our arms at Manila" does not belong in the category of
"human action" but in some other category that "overrules human action."
This other category is identified with "the march of events." Here the
Government of the United States discounts its own authority over the
march of events, conceding the sway of destiny.

---

22. *Ibid*, p. 621.

CHAPTER II

The Anatomy of Destiny

External Circumstances

> When the last gun was silenced on this memorable May day, a high authority announced the meaning of the day's work as follows: "Spain has lost her fleet and she has lost these islands also; without ships she cannot hold them, and this fleet cannot be replaced." Desperate efforts have been made by military and diplomatic methods to reverse this verdict. But history does not allow the hands of the clock to be put back, and the fact remains that the Philippine Archipelago was virtually and strategically relieved from the domination of Spain by the squadron commanded by Admiral Dewey on the first of May.
>
> —*Lieutenant C. G. Calkins, USN*

Neither our Government nor our people had planned, foreseen, or desired our acquisition of the Philippines. Finding ourselves at a point where we appeared no longer to have any choice, we saw in this the action of some power beyond our control.

Senator Beveridge, whose oratorical gifts exceeded his other endowments, was persuaded that God had "marked the American people as His chosen Nation to finally lead in the regeneration of the world."[1] A man of William Allen White's worth was equally capable of speaking

---

1. Mark Sullivan, *Our Times,* I, p. 48.

in this vein. "It is the Anglo-Saxon's manifest destiny," he said, "to go forth as a world conqueror. He will take possession of the islands of the sea. . . . This is what fate holds for the chosen people. It is so written. . . . It is to be."[2] Even Captain Mahan, who had participated notably in the development of that strategy which left us possessed of the Philippines, was moved to write: "The part offered to us is great, the urgency is immediate, and the preparation made for us, rather than by us, in the unwilling acquisition of the Philippines, is so obvious as to embolden even the least presumptuous to see in it the hand of Providence. Our highest authority, while rebuking rash judgment, rebukes also with at least equal severity the failure to read the signs of the times."[3] If, one gathers, we were driven by an outraged virtue to liberate the Cubans from Spain, it was by divine destiny that we were concurrently driven to impose our own colonial rule on the Filipinos.

The sceptical observer is tempted to reply that it was not a matter of destiny at all. We simply blundered into the possession of the Philippines by a series of actions without forethought. At no point did McKinley, Roosevelt, Lodge, Mahan, Dewey, or any of the other prime actors consider the long-range consequences of the successive decisions, each of which seemed sensible at the time in the light of immediate circumstances.

Freedom of decision was clearly ours. Our Constitution authorizes the President to conduct our foreign relations and command our armed forces. At no time in our history has the exercise of this authority been so free of constraint from other powers as in 1898. Spain never even pretended to threaten us. Our foreign and military policies were not limited by the requirements of a defensive position. On the contrary, we had the initiative. While the Spanish government and its armed forces remained moribund we, as a nation, went to war of our own free will and struck at the Spanish East Indies.

We should be wary, nevertheless, of dismissing the concept of destiny too brusquely. It was not a detached philosopher surveying these developments from a distance, as Gibbon surveyed the decline of Rome, who saw in them the workings of an historical destiny. It was the actors

---

2. *Ibid,* I, p. 50. These statements ought to be forgotten, if it were not for their usefulness in reminding us that such flights from sobriety are not confined to the Germans under Kaiser Wilhelm II, the Japanese of the 1930s, or any other nation at any other time.

3. "Effect of Asiatic Conditions," *in Problems of Asia, op. cit.,* p. 175.

themselves, those who had to resolve the dilemmas of the moment, those who presumably exercised choice in making the relevant decisions. Might one not expect that they would be the least likely to see destiny in what they had themselves chosen to do? Yet they all had this sense that destiny had been at work, that it had "ruled and overruled" them.

This is not so strange on a second look as it may be on a first. In a simple view the President of the United States, availing himself of his ample constitutional authority, uses his unfettered judgment to make the decisions that shape history, and then issues the orders which put them into effect. But no President of the United States finds this to be so in actuality. The man who occupies this office is still only one among many. He exercises greater or less leadership over the many, but even in the best of circumstances he is able to do so only by leading them in a direction in which they are disposed to go. Consequently, it is never quite clear to what extent he leads and to what extent he follows. The McKinley Administration was not a strong one and the element of followership in its behavior was considerable. As we have seen, McKinley led the country into a war with Spain because that was where it was going anyway. He submitted to "circumstances," to what perhaps was a "destiny" of sorts. And we cannot be sure that a stronger President would have been able to do otherwise.

There never was a decision to attach the Philippines to the United States until it was found that they virtually were attached already. By the time the issue was full-blown, the question which presented itself for decision was not whether we should take them but whether we should keep them. By this time, however, it was not easy for our Government or our responsible citizens to find any acceptable alternative to keeping them. Recalling the dilemma, President McKinley later told William Howard Taft of his own reluctance. "But it was the only feasible course open to us. It was impossible to avoid this responsibility. . . ."[4]

What brought us to this point was a succession of particular decisions relating solely to military operations. We ended with a commitment that we had not had at the beginning, and the first question to ask is at what point in the succession of decisions we became comitted.

4. "McKinley and Expansion," address delivered by Taft on January 29, 1908; published as a leaflet at Columbus, Ohio.

The date on which we formally and forcibly deposed the Spanish authority in the Philippines, replacing it with our own, was August 13, 1898. Until then, Spain still had a jurisdiction formally unquestioned by any government in the world, including our own, which had made an issue of her jurisdiction in Cuba only. On the preceding day, however, we had concluded in Washington an armistice or peace protocol with Spain whereby we were to occupy Manila pending a later decision on the future of the Philippines.[5] Thus we established ourselves in physical possession while making it clear that we were committed neither to keeping them ourselves nor returning them to Spain.

This left us free, in a formal sense, to decide by leisurely deliberation among ourselves what had best be done with the islands. One of the conclusions to which we might have come, presumably, was the one generally accepted by later generations, that we should take no responsibility for them, and we might have made our decision accordingly. In any case, we were free to consider the matter thoroughly in the light of our national principles, our national interests, and our obligations.

The third of these factors, however, that of our obligations, was materially changed by the fact that we were now in physical possession. One might say that before August 12 and 13 the future of the Philippines was no more our concern than was the future of the Belgian Congo. But once we had ousted Spain and taken her place the responsibility became ours. Now it was up to us to decide whether the islands should be receded, given to some other power, kept for ourselves, or left to the Filipinos. Presumably, however, we were free to make this choice. Is not freedom of decision, after all, the peculiar privilege of authority?

In fact, however, our freedom was narrowly circumscribed by our new responsibility. The man who liberates an enslaved child is not really free to decide whether he will cut its throat, leave it to die of exposure, or sell it into slavery again. In deference to his own reputation and his self-respect he must assure the welfare of the child, even though it thereby becomes a charge upon him. The meaning of responsibility implies the limitation of freedom, so that the privilege of authority is forever offset by the obligations that accompany it.

It would have been one thing to leave the islands with Spain; it was another to give them back. In the former case Spain would still have held them by virtue of Magellan's discovery, with which we had nothing

---

5. Our commanders in Manila had not yet heard about this when they captured the city.

to do; in the latter she would hold them on our responsibility. No sooner was this alternative thought of than it became unthinkable.

The alternative of independence seemed, at first, to make the best sense. The Spanish war had been conceived by our people as a war of liberation, and had been justified accordingly. While it was only the Cubans whom we had set out to liberate, by the fortunes of war we had now liberated the Filipinos as well. This had not been our intention, but it was the way everyone was now bound to interpret what had happened. Since we had liberated the Filipinos along with the Cubans, the obvious thing to do was to give them, too, the independence for which they, like the Cubans, had been struggling. It was widely assumed, even among the responsible representatives of our government, that this would be done as a matter of course. " 'Every American citizen who came in contact with the Filipinos at the inception of the Spanish war,' stated General Thomas M. Anderson, who was the first to give to Dewey the news that there was talk in the United States of the retention of the islands, 'or at any time within a few months after hostilities began probably told those he talked with . . . that we intended to free them from Spanish oppression.' "[6]

At the initiative of our consul general in Singapore, and upon Dewey's order, Emilio Aguinaldo, the leader of the Philippine independence movement, was brought to Manila from Hong Kong in an American dispatch boat on May 19. There he was given not only encouragement but material support in his efforts to overthrow the Spanish rule. As the days passed, however, it began to appear doubtful in Washington that the Filipinos were ready for self-government.

What, one must ask, is the test of such readiness? Were the Spanish Americans ready for self-government in the first quarter of the nineteenth century, when Napoleon's victory over Spain set them free? Not if one judges by the political chaos that ensued and that has persisted, in some measure, even in our own times. Was Cuba, herself, ready for self-government in 1898? Judging by the record of her domestic politics in the ensuing generations one might question it. On June 27, three days before the arrival of General Anderson, Dewey had cabled Washington: ". . . In my opinion these people are far superior in their intelligence and more capable of self-government than the natives of Cuba, and I am familiar with both races."[7]

---

6. Tyler Dennett, *Americans in Eastern Asia, op. cit.*, p. 618.
7. *Appendix to the Report of the Chief of the Bureau of Navigation, op. cit.*, p. 103. By the fall of 1899, however, when Dewey wanted to convince the

The independence movement in the Philippines, like that in Cuba, was of long standing and evidently had considerable popular support. Was it up to the United States, newly arrived on the scene, to determine now that the insurgents could not give the country a satisfactory government? Was it really to protect the Philippine people from the Filipino insurgents that we ended by fighting the insurgents and imposing our own rule? It seems strange that the same humanitarian considerations should have produced such contrary policies in Cuba and the Philippines; and if we were going to add one rather than the other to territory under our jurisdiction there are reasons why Cuba might have been preferred.

Our discovery that the Filipinos were not ready for self-government appears, in fact, to be based on another test of readiness. Between May 1, 1898, and the fall of the year, it became increasingly evident to our authorities that the Filipinos, liberated from Spain, would by themselves be unable to keep their independence. If the United States got out, Germany, Japan, France, Russia, or Britain would come in on its heels. Some of our anti-imperialists, even, who opposed our seizure of the Philippines in the great debate of the next two years, agreed that we would, in any case, have to make ourselves responsible for their defense. They argued for a sovereign and independent state which would not have to provide its own defense but could look to the United States, away across the seas, for the gratuitous performance of this service. Half a century later this conception was to be realized.[8]

President that we should "never—never" give up the islands, he told him that the Filipinos were not capable of self-government and would not be "for many, many years." (Facsimile of McKinley's memorandum of conversation, in Charles S. Olcott's *The Life of William McKinley*, Boston, 1916, Vol. II, facing page 96.)

In neither case did Dewey know what he was talking about. For one thing, the Philippines were inhabited by several distinct races, including some exceedingly primitive people, and the distinct races were associated with distinct civilizations.

8. The outstanding weakness of the anti-imperialist position, however, was that it tended to evade the question of what we should do, confining itself to what we must not do. Where all possible courses of action are bad, it is not enough to rule one of them out for no other reason. What counts is the relative badness. The more thoughtful anti-imperialists were troubled by this. Some conceded the need for a protectorate. Carl Schurz (address at the University of Chicago, January 4, 1899, published as leaflet, Boston, 1899, p. 30) suggested an international guarantee of neutrality for the islands, as in the case of Belgium and Switzerland; but this was hardly within the realm

Would-be liberators should keep in mind a lesson that has been repeatedly exemplified since 1898. When you liberate a country, intentionally or otherwise, you almost always find yourself somehow committed to the maintenance of its liberated status. You tend to become the guarantor of your own handiwork. We felt, when the moment of decision came, that we could not separate the Philippines from Spain only to have them fall into the hands of one of the other powers. If, by saving them from the wolf, we allowed them to be torn to pieces by the pack, our role would appear discreditable; we would have failed in our duty as a responsible power. The Philippines were not ready for self-government, in our eyes, primarily because they did not have that capacity for defending themselves which is one of the attributes of a truly independent sovereignty.[9]

After the Battle of Manila Bay, various powers sent naval forces to the scene to observe matters and protect the interests of their nationals. Germany maintained in the Bay a naval force greater than Dewey's, and the German commander assumed an arrogance that showed a degree of contempt for Dewey's position. This impressed us. We suspected then, what has since been confirmed, that the Kaiser's Government was, in fact, moved by a desire to get the Philippines for Germany. (That the realization of this desire would have served our self-interest better than Germany's was not apparent at the time. History is full of incidents in which nations have competed for the possession of liabilities that look like assets.) If our forces steamed away now, having unseated the Spanish authority, they would leave the forces of Germany and the other powers behind them in Manila Bay. This was unthinkable to our people and would have been discreditable in the eyes of other nations. Other powers, representing civilization, would be making good our default. By assuming for ourselves the authority of government, we had already become committed to the naval defense of a land far away across the

---

of possibility. For the most part, the anti-imperialists held their arguments to a high level of theoretical reasoning that evaded the practical problem. Their difficulty was that they embarked on their cause when what they opposed had already become virtually an accomplished fact. It was really *undoing*, rather than *not doing*, that they were advocating. But, as is generally true in international relations, undoing was impossible.

9. Dennett, *Americans in Eastern Asia, op. cit.*, p. 623.

ocean on the coast of Asia, and to the maintenance of order among the seven million turbulent people who inhabited it.[10]

It is true that the price of Cuban liberation was the same, in the sense that we were thereafter committed to the defense of Cuba. But we were already committed, if not under the Monroe Doctrine, then by our vital strategic interests, to the defense of the area within which Cuba lay. Here that defense presented no problem, partly because it was close to our home bases and partly because no other power challenged our hegemony in it. Though chaos should reign inside Cuba, no other power would be at hand to take advantage of it by establishing its rule. The opposite was true in the Philippines, which lay in a distant region that had not been marked off for us, a region in which, until 1945, other powers were to be more strongly established than we were. By assuming a responsibility for the Philippines that could not be discharged without the acquiescence of other powers, we thereby gave the acquiescing powers a hostage. By so much, our new position in the far Pacific was one of danger and weakness. Even today, when we have given the Philippines their independence, there is no practicable way by which we could rid ourselves of the responsibility for their defense.

After August 13 we had to decide whether we would give the Philippines back to Spain, allow some other power to have them, leave them to the Filipinos, or keep them for ourselves. In theoretical terms, we were free to choose. In practical terms, the first two alternatives were foreclosed. The third was virtually foreclosed as well, since it would have required us to establish a protectorate, and this, in turn, would have entailed, if it was to be effective, such rights of intervention as we retained even in Cuba under the Platt Amendment.

The only alternative left was for us to continue in possession. It is true that this last alternative might have been regarded as no less unacceptable than the other three. But it represented the existing state of things, which always has the advantage where all alternatives are equally

---

10. The anti-imperialists themselves recognized the obligation. The Democratic platform in the election campaign of 1900 stated: ". . . we favor an immediate declaration of the nation's purpose to give to the Filipinos first a stable form of government, second, independence, and third, protection from outside interference, such as has been given for nearly a century to the republics of Central and South America." *Public Opinion*, XXIX, No. 2, 7/12/00.

unacceptable. More important, at the moment it seemed far from unacceptable to what was, perhaps, a majority of our interested citizens, and to the Administration in Washington. They saw us establishing ourselves by the decree of destiny in a dominating position on the far side of the Pacific, where the cornucopia of commercial opportunities in China was about to be spilled. They tasted, by anticipation, the glory of our new eminence in the world. And all this was to come to us through no evil machinations on our part, but as the providential reward of our virtue. We were to enjoy what were, for others, the fruits of sin, while retaining our own innocence. No one, at the moment, anticipated the war we were about to fight for the subjugation of the Filipinos, with all the moral confusion that it would entail.

In retrospect, one can make a good case for it that, if we made a mistake after August 13, it was merely in not declaring our intention to prepare the Philippines for independence at the earliest possible date. By August 13 we were already committed to responsibility for their care and protection indefinitely. The commitment had already been assumed, and we must look to earlier decisions if we are to find at what point it was assumed.

$$\bullet \qquad \bullet \qquad \bullet$$

"If old Dewey had just sailed away when he smashed the Spanish fleet," McKinley is reported to have said later, "what a lot of trouble he would have saved us."[11] Before 1898 was over many of our people were to ask why Dewey did not just sail away, and to this day his failure to do so is widely regarded as the fatal omission that left the Philippines on our hands.

To have sailed away, however, would have been a course of action for which Dewey had no authority and which he could not have justified in the circumstances. His governing instructions, in the casually worded cable of February 24 from Roosevelt, were to undertake "offensive operations in Philippines" after dealing with the Spanish squadron. However vague this instruction, it clearly did not mean that he might just sail away from the Philippines after dealing with the squadron, and for him to have done so would have been in violation of it.

---

11. H. H. Kohlsaat, *From McKinley to Harding*, p. 68. Quoted by F. R. Dulles in *America's Rise to World Power*, *op. cit.*, p. 50.

How would anyone have explained to the American people, in their hour of patriotic exultation, the retirement of their victorious fleet? In the public mind, "honor" was as much the issue, now, as anything else. "Our flag" was prominent in the vocabulary of the day, and these matters were discussed in terms of alternatives between keeping it flying or "hauling it down" in the face of the enemy. Were we going to strike Old Glory after such a victory, leaving the foeman's flag still waving? Was our fleet to come skulking home, leaving Spain in occupation of the field as if the victory had been hers? A question cast in these terms was already as good as answered.

Moreover, there was at least one Spanish gunboat, perhaps more, still at large among the islands. If Dewey had just sailed away, this force, whatever it consisted of, would have remained free to attack our merchant shipping—thereby adding to the scandal.

Finally, by destroying the Spanish squadron Dewey had, to an unknown extent, impaired the governing authority in the islands. That authority had already found itself on the defensive, in the preceding years, against the Filipino insurgents. Was there any assurance that, crippled as it now was, it could still maintain order or protect the lives and property of the people of Manila, including Europeans and Americans? Apparently Dewey, himself, was mindful of a responsibility which had fallen upon him as a result of his blow to Spanish authority. Cabling Washington on May 4, he said: "Much excitement at Manila. Scarcity of provisions on account of not having economized stores. Will protect foreign residents."[12] To have just sailed away, leaving possible chaos and bloodshed in his wake, would have represented an abdication of humane responsibility for which he might later have been held accountable; and it might have given rise to circumstances in which the forcible intervention of other powers would have been justified and inevitable. Again one must ask how it could have been explained to the American people.

It is hard to avoid the conclusion that it was not politically feasible for Dewey just to sail away. Any administration that had ordered his

---

12. *Appendix to the Report of the Chief of the Bureau of Navigation, op. cit.,* p. 68. In a memorandum of August 27, 1898, written in the Philippines, Brig. Gen. F. V. Greene, U.S.V., said: "If the United States evacuate these islands, anarchy and civil war will immediately ensue and lead to foreign intervention." (Senate Document No. 62, Part 2, 55th Congress, 3d Session, Washington, 1899, p. 374.)

immediate return would have committed itself to political disaster and would be remembered in infamy to this day. It would, moreover, have been sacrificing itself for a cause of which it was not aware and which was apparent to no one in the first days of May, 1898. The historian is duty-bound to remember that men and governments can never act on the basis of knowledge and insights which are not available to them at the time, however much their successors may wish they had.

In the hour of victory it apparently occurred to no one that Dewey might sail away forthwith. This was an afterthought, born when the long-range consequences of his stay in Manila began, at last, to be visible. From the moment when the news of victory transpired, our government and the press alike assumed that we were thereby placed in possession of the Philippines. The dispatch of troops to garrison them and keep order responded to a responsibility which, presumably, had already become ours. Dewey, himself, took no different view of the situation; and, as we have seen, this view was substantially correct. The later view that we could have hit and run became plausible only as elapsing time obscured the realities.

If this is true, our commitment to responsibility for the Philippines was born in the moment when we destroyed the Spanish squadron on May 1. After that we could find no feasible way to rid ourselves of it. In our search, then, for the decision that was responsible for this commitment we ought to look at the decisions that led to the Battle of Manila Bay.

●   ●   ●

The reader should put himself in the position of any responsible American naval official confronting, in the months before April 24, 1898, the prospect of a war with Spain. The political objective of such a war would be the liberation of Cuba. But the military objective, which concerned the Navy, would be to bring Spain to a point where she was willing to submit to our will in the matter. This meant hurting her as hard as possible wherever she could be hurt until she cried out that she was ready to accept our terms. Once that had been done, the political objective of a liberated Cuba could be realized by our civilian negotiators.

If there were political reasons for limiting this effort, for not hurting Spain as much as we could or wherever we could, it was not the Navy's business to determine for itself what they might be or, on its own initiative, to be governed by them. This was the business of the President and his principal adviser on foreign policy, the Secretary of State. In the absence of any injunction from the President, the Navy's duty was to be prepared with plans for hurting Spain to the utmost. This, after all, is what the western world has conceived war to be ever since the days of Napoleon and Clausewitz when, after a century and a half, it again became a thoroughly serious matter.

The alert naval official who was responsible for plans to meet the contingency of war would naturally look for the points at which Spain was vulnerable, the exposed places. The most conspicuous of these, after Cuba and Puerto Rico, was in the Philippine archipelago, where she maintained a small, antiquated, ineffective squadron of naval vessels, one of which was of wood.

The Navy's responsibilities for the defense of our commerce on the high seas would also have to be taken into account by our imaginary naval official. The Spanish ships in the Philippines, unhindered, would be able to raid our merchantmen in the Pacific. The duty of the Navy would be to prevent this.

As a matter of routine duty, then, the naval official would make plans, first to neutralize the Spanish ships, and then to do whatever further injury to Spain could be done in her exposed Philippine possession. We have seen that plans for a Philippine campaign were, in fact, being prepared by the Navy even under the Administration of President Cleveland, whether the President knew it or not.

When Theodore Roosevelt was made Assistant Secretary of the Navy in the spring of 1897, he brought his own vitality to bear on the development of these plans. The command of our Asiatic squadron falling vacant at the end of the year, in connection with routine transfers, he had the forethought to obtain the assignment to the post of a particularly competent officer in the person of Commodore Dewey. He was concerned that, if a job was to be done in the Philippines, it be well done. At the time he could not see, as we do now, the advantage there would be in not having it too well done.

This routine war-planning was given no direction from above. Roosevelt's problem, apparently, was to get the President and the Secretary of the Navy simply to acquiesce in it.[13] What he got from them was, in fact, a rather troubled acquiescence. Perhaps they had been thinking only of a small local war, if war was to come at all.

---

13. *Cf.* Theodore Roosevelt to John D. Long, 9/20/97 and 1/14/98, *op. cit.*

The record does not show precisely to what extent the plans for a Philippine campaign were known outside the Navy Department before the outbreak of war. Senator Lodge, through his close association with Roosevelt, had taken an active interest in them; as had Mahan even before he was recalled from his retirement. Very likely they were mentioned by Secretary Long at Cabinet meetings in the presence of the Secretary of State, although this is pure conjecture. It is evident, however, that they raised an issue in nobody's mind and that no hard thought was given, consequently, to their possible political implications.

We should take note of this, because thought and decision in a government like ours is largely the product of the need to resolve issues. An issue generally has to be made in order to initiate the process. If only one man with a strong enough voice in our counsels had raised a question about the political advisability of carrying out these plans, a debate might have ensued and the consequent expenditure of thought might then have revealed the political dangers that, as it was, remained hidden. Such a question might have led to the provision of a rationale for what appear to have been the unreasoned apprehensions of the Secretary of the Navy, and probably of the President too, at the boldness of the design that Roosevelt was advancing.

For it seems to have been true that, while no one thought of any reason why we should not attack the Philippines, only the Navy thought of doing so. The public had its eyes on Cuba and was surprised by what happened across the Pacific. "Some New York papers had ventured to interpret the gathering of ships at Hong Kong to mean that they were to come to the Atlantic. The odd notion of a local war between two nations with world-wide interests still survived."[14] The notion was odder to a naval officer than it was to a public, a President, and a Secretary of the Navy who were not sophisticated in these matters.

Still, no one thought of a reason why not. It occurred to no one that there were dangerous political implications in the projected military operations; and it would have been hard to object to them over the approval of all the competent military authorities. When, on April 24, the President nodded his assent to the dispatch of the order drafted by Captain Crowninshield, he quite innocently committed the United States

---

14. Lieut. C. G. Calkins, USN, in *The American-Spanish War: A History by the War Leaders*, Norwich, Conn., 1899, p. 107.

to the acquisition of an empire on the shores of Asia. It is this decision, in particular, that we are asked to attribute to destiny.

●   ●   ●

Nothing is easier than to ridicule the notion of destiny, taking advantage alike of the wisdom afforded by our hindsight and of our detachment from the small considerations that could not be overlooked at the time. A situation can at least be imagined, however, in which there was no practicable alternative to the decision which produced the Battle of Manila Bay.

Suppose that the Spanish squadron in Manila constituted a substantial threat to our virtually undefended west coast, or was thought to constitute such a threat.[15] Could our Government have closed its eyes to that threat? Or could it have refrained from meeting it with vigor and determination? Or could it have ranged Dewey's squadron of six ships defensively off the thousand miles of our Pacific coastline? Under these circumstances, it must have been constrained to seek the promptest and surest way of neutralizing the Spanish force, even though that meant an invasion of Manila Bay and a blow to the Spanish authority in the Philippines.

If such had been the circumstances, we would have to conclude here that our commitment to responsibility for the Philippines became practically inescapable when it was decided to have a war with Spain at all. It would then be that earlier decision which we should have to examine for traces of destiny.

In point of fact, it was possible to recognize from the beginning that the Spanish squadron in Manila did not constitute a threat to our west coast. In a memorandum of January 14, 1898, to Secretary Long,[16]

---

15. Some did, in fact, regard it as such a threat. Steps were taken by the Army—even after the destruction of Spain's Pacific squadron—with a view to strengthening the west coast's defenses (cf. Adjutant General's Office, *Correspondence* . . . , *op. cit.*, II, p. 673). This may have represented merely the frenzy of zeal which the Army experienced after the Navy's triumph of May 1. Dewey tells us in his *Autobiography* (*op. cit.*, p. 229) that, when news of the victory reached the United States, "all anxiety for the safety of the Pacific coast was relieved."

16. *The Letters of Theodore Roosevelt, op. cit.*, I, p. 761.

Roosevelt wrote that, with only the four ships he then had, Dewey "could overmaster the Spanish squadron" in the Philippines. He added: "If we had trouble with any power but Spain I should not advise Hawaii [not yet in our possession] being left unprotected, but with Spain I do not think we need consider this point." The only bases the Spanish squadron had in the Pacific were Manila and Guam, and its radius of action from these bases would not have enabled it to threaten our west coast.[17]

It remains true that the Spanish squadron, unopposed, would have been free to prey on our merchant shipping in the western Pacific. Could a responsible government in Washington have abstained from doing anything about this? Could it have survived an attempt to explain its abstention to the American people if, in consequence, American lives and property were lost? What would the effect have been on American prestige abroad? As a practical matter, something surely did have to be done about this threat.

But it could have been met by less aggressive tactics than those adopted by Dewey when he ran through the entrance of Manila Bay, under the guns of the Spanish forts and without regard for possible mines, to slaughter the Spanish squadron at its anchorage. It could have been accomplished with less risk, if also less heroically, by simply blockading Manilla Bay. And this could have been done whether, upon his arrival, Dewey had found the Spanish force inside the Bay or out. That force, which could not defend itself against him under the protection of the Cavite batteries, would have been even more helpless away from them. Caught inside the Bay, it could emerge only to meet disaster. Caught outside and deprived of access to its only base, it would have found itself at an even greater disadvantage. Unless it had been strong enough to break Dewey's blockade, therefore, it could not have raided our commerce or hurt us in any other way.[18]

A blockade, moreover, would have been politically feasible. If any of our people had criticized the restraint it represented, a plausible case

---

17. *Cf.* Chadwick, *op. cit.,* I, pp. 90–91. Also *New York Herald,* March 10, 1898, p. 6, column 4.
18. While such a blockade was possible, the reader should bear in mind that considerable technical difficulties in keeping coaled and repaired would have been entailed. Cf. H. W. Wilson, *The Downfall of Spain: Naval History of the Spanish-American War,* London, 1900, p. 158. Also Sprout, *op. cit.,* p. 238.

could surely have been made for not risking our squadron in a run past the Spanish forts and through a channel that might be mined, only to give the Spaniards the advantage of supplementing the fire of their ships with that of their shore batteries. The fact that Dewey succeeded so brilliantly in these tactics obscures the fact that they might have proved foolhardly. If the Spanish gunners at the entrance to the Bay had been alert and competent, or if the channel had been effectively mined, our squadron might never have got in at all, and the history of the United States in the Far East might have taken a different turn.

A blockade would have adequately served our defensive purpose. But it would have been less effective in the service of that other purpose, which was to force Spain's submission to our will by hurting her and demonstrating her helplessness to resist us. The swift, dramatic victory in Manila Bay was the first blow struck at Spain in the War, and perhaps the most telling. When it was followed by the destruction, off Santiago, Cuba, of the only other naval force which she had committed to battle, she was ready to meet our terms. Without it she might not have given up quite so soon and the war might have been prolonged to some extent, although the same outcome could hardly have been in doubt. Spain never had a plausible chance of beating us by herself, and her desperate hopes of intervention by the European powers would hardly have been more likely of realization if we had refrained from striking down her authority in the Philippines.

One never knows for sure what might have happened in history had things been otherwise, but we may reasonably suppose that a practicable alternative to the destruction of the Spanish power in Manila was to be found in the simple containment of that power. This might well have left us free just to sail away and come home when the war was over. The islands would have remained, then, a burden and a strategic liability for Spain or for whatever other power succeeded her in their possession.[19]

● ● ●

Dewey, himself, could not have been expected, on political grounds, to make the decision to blockade rather than invade the Bay of Manila. He quite properly understood that his business was to strike Spain as

---

19. Germany, especially, with the First World War approaching, might have found that her possession of them confirmed Bismarck's wisdom in warning against the acquisition of a distant colonial empire.

hard a blow as he could. If, instead, a paramount political consideration required that he exercise military restraint, then it was up to the President to have him instructed accordingly. The President, through the Secretary of the Navy, could have ordered him to blockade the Spanish squadron but to avoid putting the power of the United States into any position in which it might find itself responsible for the government of the Philippines. We can see now that this is what he should have done.

Again, however, no one at the time saw the issue, no one weighed the alternatives of blockade and invasion in terms of their political implications.

The crucial decision was the one that dispatched Dewey to the Battle of Manila Bay. As far as external circumstances were concerned, the President had freedom of choice in making this decision. He could have made it otherwise than he did and thereby, one supposes, have avoided our acquisition of responsibility for the government of the Philippines. If he had had such foresight, however, he would hardly have been the child of his times which he in fact was. He would have been a prodigy. And one may doubt that such a prodigy, a man so far in advance of the thinking of his countrymen, would have had a better chance of being elected President in 1896 than, say, Henry Adams.

The decision that sent Dewey to Manila Bay was the President's in a formal sense. It was developed by the more or less routine activity of his subordinates in the Navy Department. Fundamentally, however, it was a product of the culture which predominated in America about the turn of the century. The President, in his policy, was simply giving expression to the common mind of the day, with all its elements of distinction and all its limitations.

CHAPTER III

The Anatomy of Destiny

Men and the Times

I find myself beset with one difficulty whenever I undertake to debate this question. I am to discuss and denounce what seems to me one of the most foolish and wicked chapters in history. Yet I am compelled to admit that the men who are responsible for it are neither foolish nor wicked.

—*George M. Hoar*

Today we can see that worldwide transformations were impending at the turn of the century. The established inter-relationships of peoples were becoming unsettled. Old concepts of international society were on the verge of obsolescence. The terms of war and peace were about to acquire a new grammar.

Those who grope through history for a prophetic understanding should note how often aspects of the human environment are consciously appreciated only when they are about to go. After the invention of steamboats, the art of sailing was accorded a devotion and development that it had not enjoyed before. The natural wilderness was never valued so highly or studied so intensively as when men found themselves beginning to conduct their lives amid the amenities of an urban existence. Schools do not offer courses in the appreciation and composition of poetry until the periods of great poetic production are over. When a society becomes self-conscious about values which it previously took for granted we may suspect that those values are losing their relevance to it.

The history of sea-power was twenty-four centuries old when Mahan became its prophet. Themistocles had first demonstrated its principles and its potency in making Athens a maritime power. It had since been exercised by a succession of maritime empires, generally after the fashion of Monsieur Jourdain's conversation before he found out that what he spoke was prose. Through the long accumulation of historic experience, its principles had eventually come to be tacitly understood and to be represented in action. But they remained unformulated and the power which was exercised on the maritime routes remained nameless until Mahan identified it as "sea-power" and wrote his explicit appreciation of it. The word of the prophet was then taken up around the globe. Nations, some of whom had practiced sea-power for centuries, began to practice it with a new self-consciousness at a moment when the intercontinental bombers and missiles were, at last, about to transcend the geographic distinction on which it rested. In the perspective of the centuries since Themistocles, it appears that Mahan's testament was a memorial rather than the celebration of a new birth.

Mahan's appreciation of sea-power was one aspect of the self-conscious imperialism that became dominant for this moment in our history, like a nova flaring out. Since the fifteenth century, the western world had been establishing its empire in the backward areas of the earth. In the Americas, in Africa, around the rim of Asia, wherever sea-power reached, the European white man had imposed his dominion over what were regarded as lesser races. It was not until now, when the age of colonial imperialism was drawing to a close, that this was rationalized and an explicit principle made of it. In England, Joseph Chamberlain admonished his countrymen to "think imperially," as if that were something new to the English rather than something that was about to become *passé*.[1] Rudyard Kipling, noting our American misgivings at the prospect of having to rule the Philippines, urged us to "take up the White Man's burden."[2] Our own expansionists represented to us the duty of the white man, or of the Anglo-Saxon, or of the civilized powers to bring light and order to the heathen in the dark

---

1. Speech at Guildhall, London, January 19, 1904; quoted in *Everyman's Dictionary of Quotations*. Prior to the period of Disraeli, at least, English imperialism had been a manifestation of absentmindedness, as John Seeley pointed out in *The Expansion of England*, London, 1925, p. 10.
2. *McClure's Magazine*, XXI, Feb., 1899, p. 291. *Cf.* Dulles, *America's Rise to World Power, op. cit.*, p. 48.

places of the earth. This was the responsibility of greatness, the obligation imposed on the mature and enlightened nations. Within our own hemisphere it took the form of Roosevelt's corollary to the Monroe Doctrine, whereby we made ourselves responsible for good behavior among the Caribbean republics.

At its best, this rationalized imperialism was sober, responsible, and unselfish. It stood opposed to the wanton exploitation of colonial peoples and upheld, instead, the obligation of the imperial powers to advance them along the paths of civilization. The concept found expression in the constructive colonial policies of Joseph Chamberlain and in our own administration of government in Haiti, Santo Domingo, Puerto Rico, and the Philippines.

The rationalization of imperialism also had roots, however, in Darwin's concept of natural selection and the survival of the fittest. The world was seen as a battlefield on which the races of mankind struggled for supremacy, the issue being survival. In this view, the alternative to keeping others under was to go under oneself. The sway of the white man all over the earth, or the predominance of the Anglo-Saxon, or the nordic, represented a biological superiority, perhaps God-given. Its maintenance was justified accordingly.

The rise of Japan, first clearly manifested in 1895, was interpreted in Darwinian terms to create that specter of the "Yellow Peril" by which the vision of so many of our prophets was disturbed. Japan had defeated China. She was soon to defeat Russia. If, now, she should organize China's hundreds of millions of people, if she should marshal the resources of the Orient, then the white portion of mankind might well be overrun by the superior numbers of Asia. Perhaps it was imperative, therefore, to establish the permanent imperial supremacy of the Western powers in the Far East.

Imperialism was also rationalized in terms of commerce. The prosperity of the newly industrialized nations, it was thought, depended on the overseas markets which were the product of imperial initiative and which depended on the maintenance of sea-power. At the turn of the century, this concept had an urgent application to the Chinese market, which the European powers, it appeared, were about to divide among themselves.

The support which an imperial policy got from these various lines of reasoning was reinforced by the self-confidence with which its progress in the preceding century had, by now, filled the Western world. History, regarded as an unbroken progress since the days when our ancestors came out of the trees, seemed ready, at last, to realize its purpose in the establishment throughout the earth of a civilization based on the moral enlightenment of the Victorian age and the wonders of science.

In our own case, there were men still living who had been born when our nation consisted of the original thirteen states lying between the continental wilderness and the Atlantic Ocean. We had shown our mettle in that expansion to the west coast which appeared, now, to have been our manifest destiny. Once this had been achieved, the terms of our thinking made it natural to ask of destiny: What next? When the Philippines came under our rule unsought, it seemed to many of us that our continued expansion was the answer. This the President recognized as the fate of a nation "on whose growth and career from the beginning the Ruler of Nations has plainly written the high command and pledge of civilization." (The Greeks had a word, *hubris,* for what this statement represented.) The fulfillment of our manifest destiny, it now appeared, had not been completed by our emergence on the west coast.

But what farther boundary was there? Possibilities that were exhilarating, if not intoxicating, came to mind. Beveridge said we were to rule the world.[3] Before the century was out, our flag was, in fact, flying over Puerto Rico, Hawaii, Samoa, Guam, and the Philippines; and our soldiers had borne it into the distant city of Peking. Five years later, as one of the great imperial powers, we committed ourselves to maintaining the sovereignty and territorial integrity of China, a land reaching back into the most remote regions of Central Asia. It was almost as if, under the impetus of manifest destiny, we had extended the Monroe Doctrine to include Mongolia, Chinese Turkestan, and Tibet.[4]

●   ●   ●

To the retrospective vision of historians in the middle of the twentieth century, all this was wrong. Our country appears to have had a night

---

3. *Cf.* Julius W. Pratt, *Expansionists of 1898,* Baltimore, 1936, p. 228. Also Dulles, *op. cit.,* p. 262.

4. In 1904 we did, in fact, undertake the defense of Tibet against British aggression—*c.f.* A. W. Griswold, *Far Eastern Policy of the United States,* New York, 1939, pp. 99–102; also my *Dream and Reality* (published in London as *American Foreign Policy*), 1959 and 1974, Chapters XVIII and XIX.

off, during which it made commitments by which it has been strategically overextended ever since. We are disposed, therefore, to blame the responsible statesmen of the time for their short-sightedness.

But is this not like damning philosophers before Christ for not being Christians? At the turn of the century our country had in commanding positions men whose grasp of international realities was unequalled since the generation of our founding fathers, and has remained unsurpassed. Yet it is these men of large vision who are identified on the historical record with the policy of expansion; while the petty and parochial minds of the day shrank from the acquisition even of such a vital strategic outpost as the Hawaiian archipelago.

One thinks of Theodore Roosevelt above all. A man of cultivation, an historian, his view of international affairs came to be broad and sophisticated. At a time when most Americans assumed that the great oceans in themselves sufficed for our security, he saw how precarious that security was in its dependence on Great Britain's diminishing ability to maintain the balance of power. He thought in terms of a world order based on the division of the globe into spheres of influence policed by the responsible powers. He foresaw that the United States would have to take an increasingly active role in maintaining the balance of power on which such a world order must necessarily be based. While he felt it essential to our security that British power survive the first World War, at the beginning of that contest he also saw, what our statesmen of a later generation failed to see, "that the smashing of Germany would be a world calamity, and would result in the entire western world being speedily forced into a contest with Russia."[5] Over half a century later, we who have hindsight must accord Theodore Roosevelt the respect due to a man who, in his foresight, was right, and for the right reasons.

This kind of thinking was, in a sense, unAmerican, as is demonstrated by the animus against the concepts of "balance of power" and "spheres of influence" which we have shown throughout our history. American statesmen have rarely if ever used these terms in public except to denounce what they stood for. But Roosevelt was a man of energy, personal magnetism, and exceptional capacity for leadership. "The suggestion occurs," wrote Simeon Strunsky, "that Roosevelt, at the height of his power, imposed himself on his countrymen rather than convinced them; that all along he was out of tune with the basic sentiment in the

---

5. Quoted by Edward Buehrig, *Woodrow Wilson & the Balance of Power,* Bloomington, Ind., 1955, p. 154.

country, and that this sentiment asserted itself once he had stepped from the scene at Washington."[6]

Roosevelt was also a man of extraordinary weaknesses. His intellectual sophistication was matched, in some respects, by his immaturity. His realism was matched by his romanticism. Addicted to the glories of sanguinary combat as a means of demonstrating virility, his large vision tended repeatedly to be clouded by callow dreams. He was quite carried away, for example, by the personal pride he felt at having killed a Spaniard in combat during the Cuban campaign; and he attached inordinate importance to being given a medal for heroism. He was rather generally disposed to extend this personal romanticism to national policy. His judgment as a statesman was, on occasion, overridden by his judgment as an adventurer. It is hardly possible to escape the implication in some of his remarks that the ideal of his youthful daydreams, at least, was an American garrison state carrying Old Glory at the end of a bayonet to inferior breeds across the seas. At the turn of the century, though not later, he represented the national disposition of the moment to associate patriotism with arrogance on the international scene. His mind, moreover, was always susceptible to the violence of partisanship. In spite of his wisdom, whenever his sober mind was in the ascendent, Theodore Roosevelt was not one to retain his sobriety at a moment when the rest of the country drank deep of glory. One regrets that the reputation of so great a man should have been so marred by himself.

Mahan was, on the whole, a lesser figure. But he, too, had the large vision. He saw the power relationships of the world and their precariousness. He saw that the United States would at last have to become mindful of its own security, since it could not count on the continued supremacy of Great Britain's beneficent power over the surrounding oceans. Because our country must now achieve a naval power of its own, to support and supplement that of Britain if not to take its place, he was concerned to make explicit, for our inexperienced understanding, those principles of naval action which had long been tacitly understood by the English.

One of the ironies of history is that his educational endeavor had, to our detriment, more effect on the Germans and the Japanese than on us. He was a prophet with somewhat less honor in his own country. His work gave notable impetus to naval competition abroad; but when

---

6. "Theodore Roosevelt & the Prelude to 1914," *Foreign Affairs,* Vol. IV, No. 1, October, 1925, p. 146.

Mahan's friend, Roosevelt, left office and lost his influence, our country, committed to the defense of the Philippines and the territorial integrity of China, depending for its security on the failure of the German and Japanese challenges to British sea-power, forgot about its unwanted commitments, sank back in the comfortable notion that the oceans were impassable to its enemies, and neglected its Navy. It returned to the old isolation. After its night out it slept deep. Meanwhile Germany, whose interests as a land-power surely required that she not dissipate her strength on the seas, read Mahan and dreamed of deposing Britain from Neptune's throne; while Japan read Mahan and was encouraged to develop further that power by which our newly achieved and undefended position in the Far East was to be increasingly challenged.

Mahan's greatness was in rationalizing and applying the historic experience of sea-power. His weakness was that of the successful dogmatist who conceives, at last, that the world in all its manifestations represents his dogma. In his later writings he was tempted always to continue beyond the truth into that realm in which theory reigns peerless and unconfirmed. He lacked the graces of humor and humility which might have saved him from the pompousness of those prophecies that cannot be read, today, without embarrassment and regret.

Roosevelt's faults were youthful, so that he tended to grow in wisdom with the years. Mahan's wisdom diminished with age and acclaim. In these two men, however, we had at the turn of the century a scale of vision and an appreciation of realities that had not existed in Washington since 1823, and was not to exist there for at least another generation.

Senator Henry Cabot Lodge of the Foreign Relations Committee completes the triumvirate that conspired, at this time, to engage our country in a program of imperialistic expansion. He was not the intellectual peer of the other two, but great, rather, in the influence he exercised on our policy. To those who feel that this influence exceeded the wisdom behind it, he exemplified the fact that the best education, by itself, is not enough to make a statesman. In him, rather than in Roosevelt or Mahan, we see the father of that faction which, in the inner conflict on foreign policy that was to divide us for half a century after 1898, advocated that we maintain an independent policy in the world, dissociated from the policies of other powers.

At the turn of the century, Roosevelt, Mahan, and Lodge were agreed on a program of what they called "expansion": the development of our Navy, the acquisition of overseas bases, and the active exertion of American power abroad. Roosevelt and Mahan, however, interpreted this to imply the assumption by us of a share in that responsibility for maintaining international order which had, since 1814, been an obligation of the great powers acting more or less in concert. Our achievement of maturity as a powerful nation, in their minds, did not render abstention from imperialism any more obsolete than it did the self-denying provisions of the Monroe Doctrine. Lodge, however, thought we could embrace imperialism in parts of the world where our influence was not paramount and still abstain from compromising ourselves with other powers.[7]

Of McKinley nothing would need to be said here except for the fact that he was President. The people had chosen a representative American rather than a leader in the active sense. He was of good character and a modest man. It is to his credit that he had no views on what he did not understand. He was always willing to pursue the course to which there was no alternative. When he saw that we were going to war with Spain, he called for war with Spain; and when he saw that we were expanding he became an expansionist.

These men—Roosevelt, Mahan, Lodge, McKinley—were manifestly imperfect, like the best of men in all times. Those of us who would have done better at their jobs, given the horizons that limited their vision, can afford to disdain them. The fact is that not one of them saw what we were getting into when we struck at the Philippines.

On the other side you have the anti-imperialists, including such distinguished figures as Senator Hoar, Carl Schurz, and William Graham Sumner, in addition to William Jennings Bryan. By the verdict of the historians they were right, in the sense that not acquiring the Philippines would have been better than acquiring them. But they were right in abstract principle at best, and almost entirely for what have since proved

---

7. In this he was less shrewd than the English *Saturday Review,* which in its issue of December 3, 1898, pointed out that the American peace negotiators who were providing for Spain's cession of the Philippines to us were "making their bargain—whether they realise it or not—under the protecting naval strength of England. And we shall expect, to be quite frank, a material *quid pro quo* for this assistance. We shall expect the States to deal generously with Canada in the matter of tariffs; we shall expect to be remembered when she comes into her kingdom in the Philippines; above all, we shall expect her assistance on the day, quickly approaching, when the future of China shall come up for settlement. For the young imperialist has entered upon a path where she will require a stout friend. . . ."

to be the wrong reasons.[8] The imposition of our rule in the Philippines was, as they saw it, tyrannical; and if we practised tyranny abroad we would end by practising it at home.

The historian today cannot accept these arguments, not because they were implausible but because they were not borne out. The anti-imperialists did not anticipate that our authority in the Philippines, imposed by tyrannical means, would in its continuance be lacking in tyranny. They fell into the error of expecting, in the world of reality, such consistence as gave distinction to the microcosms of their own minds. Once we had pacified the Philippines by brute force, however, we applied ourselves to the task of governing them in the spirit of our own institutions. We devoted ourselves to good works, the establishment of human rights, and the preparation of the natives for that self-government which they now enjoy. This did not corrupt us. On the contrary, if anything it bore out Roosevelt's later view that we benefitted ourselves morally by the creditable manner in which we discharged our responsibility.[9] Our record in the Philippines is, today, a source of moral self-confidence to all Americans. The anti-imperialists were wholly wrong in their wholly plausible apprehensions.

The retrospective argument against our acquisition of the Philippines, unlike the argument of the anti-imperialists, is made entirely on grounds of strategic self-interest. If Dewey had just sailed away, supposing that had been possible, the cause of tyranny would have been served; the fate of the Filipinos would have been worse. But ours would have been better. We would not have become strategically overextended. We would not have given a hostage to the rising sun of Japan or established ourselves in a position where our commitments could hardly be reconciled to her own requirements for defense in the circumstances of the twentieth century.[10] Although the Japanese, no more

---

8. *Cf.* Fred H. Harrington, "The Anti-Imperialist Movement in the United States, 1898–1900," in *Mississippi Valley Historical Review,* Vol. XXII (September, 1935), pp. 211–212.

9. Theodore Roosevelt, *Autobiography,* New York, 1914, pp. 516–517.

10. As Harold & Margaret Sprout put it: ". . . an American fleet, strong enough to guarantee security to the Philippines, could destroy the Japanese Navy and blockade Japan. On the other hand, a fleet that could defend the Japanese homeland against the United States would constitute a standing menace to the security of the Philippines." *The Rise of American Naval Power,* Princeton, 1939, p. 256.

foresighted than the rest of us, favored our acquisition of the Philippines in 1898 because of the more threatening alternatives, the destruction of the Spanish authority on May 1 set the stage for that long contest between the United States and Japan in the Pacific which, presumably, would otherwise have been no more inevitable than a contest with Britain in the Atlantic, in the absence of any assumption by us of responsibility for the independence of Ireland.

Because reality is more various and changeable than our verbal categories, the historian is constantly confronted with verbal paradoxes. Theodore Roosevelt, at the turn of the century, was chief of the expansionists. But in the longer view of his career we find him on the other side. The realistic strategic thinking that today identifies our acquisition of the Philippines as what S. F. Bemis termed the "Great Aberration of 1898" was native to him. Watching the sun of Japan rising in the East, he wanted to see us relieved, if that could be decently managed, of any responsibility for the Philippines. Even the romantic Roosevelt of the first days seems to have had some reservations about the advantage to us of the role which circumstances and duty, in his view, imposed on us. These reservations had become anxieties of the realistic Roosevelt by 1905, with the Japanese defeat of Russia. By 1914, he was clear in his desire to see us depart entirely from "the Asiatic coast." "I hope," he wrote, ". . . that the Filipinos will be given their independence at an early date and without any guarantee from us which might in any way hamper our future action or commit us to staying on the Asiatic coast. . . . Any kind of position by us in the Philippines merely results in making them our heel of Achilles if we are attacked by a foreign power. . . . If we were to retain complete control over them and to continue the course of action which in the past sixteen years has resulted in such immeasurable benefit for them, then I should feel that it was our duty to stay and work for them in spite of the expense incurred by us and the risk we thereby ran. . . . If the Filipinos are entitled to independence, then we are entitled to be freed from all the responsibility and risk which our presence in the islands entails upon us."[11] Thus Roosevelt, swayed in his youth by adventure and destiny, was ultimately in the camp of those who viewed our momentary indulgence with misgivings if not disapproval.

---

11. *New York Times*, Nov. 22, 1914. Quoted in *Theodore Roosevelt Cyclopaedia*, Albert Bushnell Hart and Herbert Ronald Ferleger, eds, New York: Roosevelt Memorial Association, 1941.

Some anti-imperialists of the turn of the century, it is true, saw the strategic considerations, and used them to supplement the arguments which they made on grounds of maintaining our republican institutions. "Who will deny," said Carl Schurz, "that if we expand territorially, especially in the Far East, we shall at once become involved in the quarrels and jealousies of the old-world nations that are competing there for colonial acquisition with constant danger of armed collision?"[12] This, however, was little more than a reminder of the self-denying provisions of the Monroe Doctrine. Others expressed misgivings at the size and cost of the Navy we would now need, making play with the endlessly expandable argument of the expansionists that the possession of sea-power required colonies, while the possession of colonies required sea-power. But that is as far as anyone appears to have gone with the strategic argument. It remained uncrystalized, imprecise, and incidental. No American really saw, at the time, what has become so clear in the retrospective view.[13]

•   •   •

How shall we pass judgment, then, on the men and events of 1898?

When the sun sank on the first of May, the future of the Philippines had become ours to determine. History appears to have justified the expansionists of the day, given the situation as it existed at the close of May 1. The fault was of earlier date.

During the week before May 1, everyone knew that Dewey was on his way to challenge the naval power of Spain in the Philippines. Still, no one saw the large significance of that action, the consequences of success in it. It was regarded as merely a military exploit. The day after its successful accomplishment, however, everyone appears to have awakened to its significance, or at least to the fact that it was of significance in the largest sense.[14]

Did Roosevelt himself, or the naval officers who participated in the planning, have any inkling before May 1 of what it portended?

Who knows what dreams and notions cross men's mind when they

---

12. "Our Future Foreign Policy," Address of August 18, 1898, printed as leaflet, p. 12.
13. Or, if he did, his voice was not heard or, heard, not heeded. One must be wary of saying what was not in any of seventy-five million minds.
14. See account of newspaper reactions in *The Literary Digest,* May 14, 1898.

are idle—which is to say, when they are thoughtful to themselves? The Navy was keenly aware of the disadvantage it suffered in having no Far Eastern base. Dewey had been forced to leave Hong Kong by British neutrality on April 24, and if he had not had an enemy base to attack he would have had no other place to go, legitimately, short of Hawaii or California. It must have occurred to people in the Navy Department, however casually, that the capture of Manila might solve this problem for the future. Who knows that Roosevelt or Lodge, musing upon these matters, did not dream of a destiny which showed the stars and stripes flying forever over the Philippines? Perhaps they went on to picture the discomfiture of their opponents, who were too timid to contemplate taking even Hawaii. It may be that, if someone had called Roosevelt's attention to the danger that his plans might result in our permanent acquisition of the Philippines, he would, in the face of that possibility, have retained his serenity.

The record, however, shows nothing of the essentially irresponsible visions that drift through the corridors of men's minds after the lights are out. It shows only that no one gave the problem, which was in everyone's mind on May 2, any overt and responsible thought before that date. It shows that Dewey's move on the Philippines was regarded as an act of war, not an act of politics, serving a purely military purpose. Those concerned with winning the war were disposed, as is so often the case, to put victory first and postpone any concern for post-war problems until after its achievement. Roosevelt, one gathers, was not looking any further. The fact that the Army had not been alerted to follow up the projected naval action stands in evidence. Indeed, it is eloquent.

The Secretary of State, at the time, was approaching senility. He resigned when we went to war. If the plans for a Philippine campaign were mentioned at a Cabinet meeting, Secretary Sherman would, perhaps, not have been the man to grasp their political significance. But let us imagine that, instead, the Secretary of State was a man whose thought was ahead of his time, whose grasp of power politics exceeded Bismarck's, whose understanding of international relations surpassed Churchill's, and who had made a hobby of the problems that beset nations when they undertake to conclude a war by making a peace. He already saw what Roosevelt saw a decade later; he had already attained the wisdom that Walter Lippmann and George Kennan, reading the lessons of our subsequent experience, were to make explicit half a century later.

Even though the projected naval operations in the Pacific had not been worth mentioning at a Cabinet meeting, there would have been other occasions for this Secretary to consider the danger and disadvantage of acquiring the Philippines. Perhaps he saw the dispatches which Oscar F. Williams, our Consul in Manila, was addressing to the Third Assistant Secretary of State.[15] Williams was frustrated because Washington was giving all its attention to the situation in Cuba while paying no attention to the like situation in the Philippines. It was hardly communicating with him at all. He wanted equality of recognition. What was happening in the Philippines was just as worthy of the headlines as what was happening in Cuba. On February 22, 1898, he wrote: "Conditions here and in Cuba are practically alike." He gave excited accounts of a Spanish reign of terror affecting even the Americans in Manila, and said that the whole Philippine population was on the verge of an uprising. Still Washington paid no attention, being as much obsessed as ever with the Cuban horrors.[16] By March 27, Williams was frantic and called for intervention. "The American Indians would not permit one of their tribes to practice such barbarities," he wrote. "Why should so-called Christian nations decline to call a halt upon Spanish outrages?"

If our imaginary Secretary of State saw these dispatches, he did not, perhaps, take them without a grain of salt. Williams, plainly, was trying to get for his post some of the limelight that now shone exclusively on Consul Lee's post in Havana. When the Secretary thought about intervening to take over the Philippines, in addition to Cuba, his spontaneous reaction was expressed in the exclamation: "Good Lord, that's all we need now!"

In the *New York Herald* for March 10, however, he happened to see a dispatch from Washington that did give him pause. "Having in view the wresting from Spain of the Philippine Islands in the event of hostilities," it began, "the naval authorities are considering a proposition to greatly strengthen the Asiatic squadron." He experienced a momentary discomfort at that phrase, "the wresting from Spain of the Philippine Islands," and his first reaction was to deplore the dramatic language

---

15. Three of these are printed in Adjutant General's Office, *Correspondence . . ., op. cit.,* II, pp. 650–653.

16. It was not until May 17, after the Army had begun to seek information on the Philippines, that the Department of State even bothered to transmit copies of these dispatches, dated from February 22 to March 27, to the Secretary of War.

which even the respectable press sometimes allowed itself to use. His second thought, however, was that this might well represent just what those navy fellows had in mind.

A dozen such possibilities of trouble come up during the normal working day of any Secretary of State. But he could not quite dismiss this one from his mind. It kept returning at odd moments. For example, he thought rather wryly of the possibility that, in the absence of a colonial office, his Department would be expected to set up a civil government in the Philippines.

This line of speculation came up again when he thought of the peace-settlement at the end of a war with Spain—if such a war should come. We couldn't just give the Philippines back to Spain, he supposed, or there'd be a howl throughout the nation. Probably we'd have to liberate them, along with Cuba. He thought of the possible consequences for law and order in Manila if those Malays and Negritos, or whatever they were, tried to set up a government and run it.

Later he recalled the German fleet under Prince Henry, the Kaiser's brother, poking about the China Sea—just looking for "a bay," as they said. Who would stop them from steaming up and taking Manila Bay after the war? That would put them right in the middle of things out there, where they wanted to be. Or the British might try to get there first. Or the French. Or the Japanese—if they dared. You could have the makings of a thumping war in the Far East. In any case, it wouldn't look well for the United States to liberate the Philippines so that they could be added to somebody else's empire.

The more the Secretary thought about this the less he was sure we could stay out of any proposals for the future of the islands after we had set them free from Spain. The whole business was speculative at best—no doubt he was looking much too far ahead now, instead of concentrating on the business in hand—but the Navy would want to keep a base in the Philippines, the Protestant missionary societies would be wanting to go out and save the souls of the Igorots, and our boy orator, Beveridge, would be wrapping himself and the Philippines up in the flag together.

Like as not, he thought, we would just have to take the islands for ourselves, and damn the consequences. Hoar, Bryan, and the rest (including the Supreme Court) would be presented with a *fait accompli*. . . . Then we would have no choice about building a big navy and annexing Hawaii. So good might come of it after all.

But he couldn't quite damn the consequences. He pictured our little Asiatic squadron charged with the responsibility of defending the new territory against all the big naval powers on the other side of the Pacific. It was clear that we would have to look to the British for support, and probably make concessions for it. . . .

●   ●   ●

If the reader wishes to go on with this fantasy he may picture our prophetic Secretary of State foreseeing the rise of Japan, which was already building itself a real navy, and possible trouble from that quarter. But, after the Secretary had exercised all this foresight, he would still have the problem of what to do about his forebodings. They had too speculative a basis to carry much conviction with the President or anyone in the Cabinet, depending as they did on a long series of *ifs*. The eventualities they dealt with were really too remote and uncertain to get anybody in Washington seriously worried. Most people would be glad to point out that we probably weren't going to have a war with Spain anyway, and that, if we did, the first order of business would be to win it, before we began worrying about what to do with the spoils.

It is not inconceivable, however, that this imaginary Secretary might have convinced the President, who had his own unreasoned misgivings, that we ought to exercise some caution not to get ourselves entangled with the future of the Philippines. The President might then, we may suppose, have had an order issued for Dewey simply to keep watch on the Spanish squadron in Manila and blockade it, but to avoid any action that might leave us with responsibility in the islands. This would not have been easy for the President. His naval advisers might well have taken the position that it was not technically possible to blockade the Philippines with a naval force seven thousand miles from its nearest base. Where would its ships go for coaling and repair?[17] The President would somehow have had to force a solution to this problem; but with sufficient will on his part and on the part of the Navy it could have been done. He would have found other difficulties as well. Roosevelt and Lodge would have been upset. Perhaps Roosevelt would have resigned. (He had already remarked that the President had no more backbone than a chocolate éclaire.) But it is just conceivable that such

---

17. Actually, Dewey had concluded secret arrangements for supplying his ships and making temporary repairs at an isolated locality on the Chinese coast, in disregard of rules of neutrality which China would be unable to enforce; but no one in Washington knew this (Dewey, *op. cit.,* pp. 188–190).

an order could have been issued, and we could have been saved from possession of the Philippines, if one man in a key position had enjoyed such foresight as we have here imagined, plus the gift of persuasion.

We cannot dismiss as a coincidence, however, the fact that, with all the ability and wisdom available in Washington in 1898, no one did have the foresight. Was there, perhaps, something of destiny about this? Perhaps our maturity as a nation had not reached that pitch at which it was possible for us to produce such thought as would have enabled us to apprehend the dangers ahead. And, because we were not really an immature nation as nations go, it may be that mankind itself was not sufficiently advanced.

We might also have kept from getting involved in the Philippines, however, if we had been a less eager, alert, and dynamic nation. A moribund government like that of Spain would not have seized the initiative as we did in the Philippines. Apparently Spain's naval command had not even read Mahan, or had not digested him, although all other naval commands supposedly had. What ships could be spared from Europe, Spain dispatched to stand on the defensive in Santiago de Cuba, rather than to threaten our coasts. She neglected to reinforce her squadron in Manila till after the news of its destruction, when she sent reinforcements as far as Suez, thought better of it, and recalled them. The cruiser *Charleston* was able to seize Guam in the Ladrones without bloodshed almost two months after the outbreak of war because the Spanish governor had not been informed of the war and the island's defenses were, in any case, out of order.[18] If we had been as sluggish and inept as Spain, the war, had there been one, would surely have been confined to Cuba. But, just as we could not exercise a foresight transcending our human limitations, so we could not escape the consequences of the energy, the drive, and the thoroughness which we regard as national virtues. Our attack on the Philippines showed a native foresight that was both too great and too little.

This being the case, perhaps it was our inescapable destiny to realize the consequences in the Far East of our own human limitations and our national virtues as they existed in 1898. For us, as we were, there may indeed have been no alternative. If this is so, then it was of the destiny inherent in our own nature that the President had been the agent.

The tragedy of human history is intrinsic in the limitations of humankind. At our best, we men have more energy than wisdom.

---

18. See Chapter IV following.

CHAPTER IV:

Sequelai

Already America has been drawn into war over the
dismemberment of one dying civilization; and it cannot
escape the conflict which must be waged over the carcass
of another. Even now the hostile forces are converging on
the shores of the Yellow Sea: the English and the
Germans to the south; Russia at Port Arthur, covering
Peking; while Japan hungers for Corea, the key to the
great inlet. The Philippine Islands . . . seem a
predestined base for the United States in a conflict which
probably is as inevitable as that with Spain. It is in vain
that men talk of keeping free from entanglements. Nature
is omnipotent; and nations must float with the tide.
                        —*Brooks Adams, August, 1898*

History is made in the dark, and those who make it cannot tell what
the illumination of after times will show to have been important.

Before the end of 1898, the Navy Department had published the
documents relating to the capture of Guam under the heading: "Seizure
of the Ladrone Islands."[1] The fact is that we had not seized the Ladrone
Islands, but the Navy officials must have supposed that their acquisition
was implicit in our capture of Guam, the seat of their government.

At the time of the Spanish American War, the most extensive island
groups between Hawaii and the Philippines, five thousand miles apart,
were in the hands of Spain, under the jurisdiction of the Governor

---

1. *Chief, Bureau of Navigation, op. cit.,* p. 151.

General of the Philippines. Parallel to our line of communication and somewhat to the south, the Carolines and Palaus stretched out for some two thousand miles. The Ladrones (or Marianas, as they are also called) cut across that line in a barrier reaching from the western Carolines toward Japan. Anyone conversant with naval strategy, one supposes, would have seen that, if we were going to be responsible for the defense of the Philippines, we had to have at least a potentially dominating position in these islands, which, while the war lasted, were ours for the taking. The fact that we let them pass through our fingers is further evidence that the Navy itself had not adjusted its thinking to the possibility that the defense of the Philippines might become our responsibility. It suggests that Mahan, himself, who was serving on the Navy's board of strategy, had not anticipated it. Naval officers would be expressing their poignant regret at this oversight before the year was out, and for many years to come.[2]

The order to capture Guam appears to have been incidental to those plans for the dispatch of troops to Manila which were made so hurriedly when news of Dewey's victory reached Washington on May 2. For some reason, it was thought necessary to convoy the first troop transports, even though the Spanish fleet had been destroyed. The cruiser *Charleston,* Captain Glass, was ordered to rendezvous with them at Honolulu. Glass was given a sealed order, dated May 10, which he opened at sea on June 4. It told him to proceed with the transports to Manila, adding:

> On your way, you are hereby directed to stop at the
> Spanish Island of Guam. You will use such force as may
> be necessary to capture the port of Guam, making
> prisoners of the governor and other officials and any
> armed force that may be there. You will also destroy any
> fortifications on said island and any Spanish naval vessels
> that may be there, or in the immediate vicinity. These
> operations at the Island of Guam should be very brief,
> and should not occupy more than one or two days.[3]

---

2. *Cf.* "Statement of Commander R. B. Bradford, U.S.N., Oct. 14, 1898, before the United States Peace Commission at Paris," Senate Document No. 62, Part 2, 55th Congress, 3d Session, Washington, 1899, pp. 472–490. Also Capt. A. S. Barker to Long, April 8, 1899 (*Papers of John Davis Long, op. cit.,* p. 247).

Captain Glass arrived at Guam June 20, fired some shots over an abandoned fort to get the range, and was thereupon visited by two Spanish officers who were surprised to learn of the war. His mission was simplified by the fact that the island's defenses were not in operating order. A courteous exchange of letters took place that same day between Glass and the Governor. The Governor wrote to say that he had been informed, by the captain of the port, "that you have advised him that war has been declared between our respective nations, and that you have come for the purpose of occupying these Spanish islands." But Glass had no instructions to occupy the islands. By way of reply, he demanded, "in compliance with the orders of my Government, . . . the immediate surrender of the defenses of the Island of Guam, with arms of all kinds, all officials and persons in the military service of Spain now in this island."[3] So the Governor, instead of surrendering the Ladrones, simply surrendered himself, his staff on the island, his arms, and the island's defenses. The convoy continued on to Manila.

As we look back, it is apparent that, if Dewey was too aggressive, Glass was too restrained.

Spain, having lost the Philippines, was left, still, with most of the Micronesian islands on her hands. She began to negotiate with Germany for their sale and, two days before the formal conclusion of the Spanish American War, on the very day that we found ourselves plunged into a new war against the Filipinos, Germany agreed to pay twenty-five million pesetas for the Palaus, the Carolines, and the Ladrones except Guam.[4]

At the end of World War I, these islands, together with the Marshalls, were taken from Germany and mandated to Japan. Japan fortified them and, in 1941, launched from them the surprise attack on Pearl Harbor. We found ourselves cut off from the Philippines, which we promptly lost, regaining them only after three and a half years, when we had fought our way back through these same islands in the campaign that ended at Hiroshima and Nagasaki.

Two orders issued by the Navy Department in 1898 had an importance that was not appreciated at the time. The character of the first

---

3. *Ibid*, p. 154.
4. *Cf.* Leslie W. Walker, "Guam's Seizure by the United States in 1898," *Pacific Historical Review,* XIV (1945), pp. 1–12; and Pearle E. Quinn, "The Diplomatic Struggle for the Carolines, 1898," *ibid,* pp. 290–302.

was determined by our national and human nature. But the character of the second was shaped more casually, representing, perhaps, simply the carelessness of busy men. Our failure to take Saipan, Truk, and the rest of Spanish Oceania was an oversight.

Epilogue

Commenting on the growth of the British Empire, at a time when it had reached its greatest expansion, Sir John Seeley remarked that the English seemed to have conquered it in "a fit of absence of mind."[1] It would be misleading to apply the term "empire" to the expansion of American power in the Far East, beginning in 1898, because it was only in the Philippines that the United States ever possessed a Far Eastern empire in the formal sense of the term. Nevertheless, the increasing American involvement in the Far East, for the first six decades of the twentieth century, entailed commitments, and consequent responsibilities, similar to those of a nineteenth-century imperial power—commitments and responsibilities that it assumed unaware.

The American nation, in its expansion, thought of itself as a liberator, spreading freedom. Indeed, this is what it did do in the Philippines, however paradoxically, after two years of a nightmarish war to subdue them, a war far greater than the Spanish-American War. It would be hard to find any more creditable record of colonial administration than what followed. The nation spent freely for the economic and social development of the Philippines, which consequently constituted an economic as well as a strategic liability for it. This, together with ideological considerations, made it eager to grant Philippine independence, as it was finally able to do in 1946. (Whether the rank-and-file of Filipinos have been better off since is a question for political philosophers.)

The unexpected and unwanted acquisition of a trans-Pacific empire

---

1. *The Expansion of England,* 1883, republished 1925, London, p. 10.

in 1898, as the result of a war over Cuba, had a momentarily intoxicating effect on the American nation. It drank deep of glory. It tended, in its innocence, to see itself as the apostle of freedom throughout the world, destined to spread its dominion, including its moral dominion, around the globe. Under the circumstances, the commitment to the defense of the Philippines was soon dwarfed by a commitment to nothing less than the defence of all China, including Manchuria and even remote Tibet. At the turn of the century, in the famous succession of "Open Door" notes, addressed to the encroaching imperial powers that had established their respective "spheres of influence" in China, the American nation committed itself to preserving China's "territorial and administrative entity." It thereby proclaimed something like a Monroe Doctrine for the other side of the world.

This quixotic commitment, which the country lacked the means to fulfill, nevertheless required it to oppose and try to thwart the Japanese incursions into China in the 1930s, a course of action that led to the Pacific war of 1941 to 1945.[2]

Even if the nation had not, just at this moment, blundered into the Far Eastern arena, the period in which it could safely abstain from participation in overseas power-politics would still have reached its end about this time. The luxury of its previous abstinence had not been made possible, as Americans generally believed, by the mere existence of the great oceans that flanked it, but by the *Pax Britannica,* which was coming to a close with the century it had dominated. Only British sea-power, commited to the objective of preventing the contestants for empire from carrying their contests into the New World, had made those oceans the protective barriers they had so far been for the United States. Now, however, that power was being challenged by the growing power of Germany and Japan. In a few years the threat that Germany would make itself dominant on the far side of the Atlantic, and so be in a position to replace British sea-power on that ocean, would draw American power across it to prevent what could no longer be prevented otherwise. On the far side of the Pacific Japan would, from the beginning, implicitly threaten the position of the United States in the Philippines and defy it in the responsibility it had so casually assumed for the defence of China.

---

2. I have told how all this came about in chapters XVIII through XX of my *Dream and Reality,* New York, 1959 (reprint editions 1973 and 1974), published in London as *Aspects of American Foreign Policy,* 1959.

It was also at the end of the century, in the 1890s, that the United States completed its expansion across the continent, that the westward-moving frontier at last disappeared, leaving it with two coasts to defend. But the only overseas threat to the Pacific coast (which had, after all, come into its possession as early as 1848), that of the Russian Empire, had already been ended long before. On the far side of the Pacific there was no power capable of spreading out over it and threatening the United States except the benign power exercised by Britain under the *Pax Britannica*. For as far ahead as anyone could see, control of the Hawaiian Islands, with an adequate naval force based upon them, was all that would be needed to insure the security of the west coast. The security of the British Isles, the security of the Hawaiian Islands, and security to the south of the United States—these represented the essential requirements of American security as the twentieth century opened. In terms of that security, responsibility for the Philippines or for China could only be a dangerous liability.

With the conclusion of World War II by the defeat of Japan in 1945, leaving the western European powers exhausted, the American nation finally had to face specific worldwide responsibilities such as no other nation had borne before—and to face them in terms, not of garnering glory but of dealing with intractable strategic realities. So, after a moment of uncertainty, it embarked on the policy of "containment," the policy of restoring or preserving a worldwide balance of power by containing what the author of the policy, George Kennan, called "Russian expansive tendencies." This, however, became transmuted, in the common mind of Americans, to the containment of "Communism," or of anything that called itself "Communism." So the American nation would again become overextended by trying to put down any movement or régime that bore the label, if only on the theory that whatever bore the label must represent "Russian expansive tendencies." It therefore committed itself to the containment of Mao Tse-tung's China (which was basically hostile to Russia), making a protectorate of Taiwan by interposing its naval power in the Straits of Formosa, and to an increasing military intervention in Vietnam, whose nominally Communist forces (really nationalistic) were far from being mere agents of Moscow.

When we look back on the overseas expansion of American power, which began on May 1, 1898, we see that it did not at any time represent a deliberate intention of territorial expansion by either the nation or its government. When the United States destroyed the Spanish power in the Philippines it did not do so with any intention of taking them for itself. Again, when it made itself the protector of Taiwan in 1950, the President explained that it was doing so only for the duration of the military emergency created by the North Korean attack on South Korea. Finally, when it began to give incidental assistance to the Government that the French had set up in Saigon it had no thought of assuming, against the opposition of half the Vietnamese people, the power of command over half Vietnam. Its motive was not imperialistic. Indeed, it was anti-imperialistic!

We have seen how, beginning in 1898, the United States became overextended in the Far East. This is to say that it found itself with commitments far beyond the resources it had for meeting them. Again after 1945 it would become overextended in the Far East, simply by commiting itself to containing or putting down any movement that bore the Communist label—even a basically nationalistic movement like that for the liberation of Vietnam from French colonial rule. And so, for a second time, it became overextended, dramatically so in Vietnam, where military victory was to be had only by a total military commitment, perhaps entailing even the use of nuclear weapons. (It would, indeed, have been possible for the American government to have adopted the policy the Romans were accused of adopting in Britain, that of making a desert and calling it peace; but this was unthinkable, if only because it would have turned the whole world, including the American people, against it in a paroxysm of horror.) The result was a reaction against such overseas commitment among the American people themselves, and the defeat of the entire American enterprise in Vietnam, entailing the necessary but morally repugnant abandonment by the United States of its Vietnamese allies.

In the history of American expansion, two dates mark the major turning-points. One is 1898, when the United States, without having intended anything of the sort, first assumed an imperial commitment across the Pacific. The other is 1973, when it finally renounced the continued expansion of its Far Eastern commitment by accepting defeat in Vietnam.

January 23, 1973, the date on which the United States concluded the agreement whereby it withdrew from Vietnam, marks the other turning-point—leading at last, one hopes, to the establishment of a balance between its capacities (political no less than military) and its commitments, one that might provide for the stabilization of its position in the world.

● ● ●

Because public discussion of the matters dealt with in this book has usually been conducted in pharisaical terms, I am tempted to end on an antipharisaical note.

To the extent that the United States, beginning in 1898, did badly in the Far East, the fault was predominantly that of a blindness universally shared by the American people and their leaders. Many books and articles have attempted to show that the acquisition of the Philippines, for example, was the consequence of a wicked plot by Theodore Roosevelt, acting in collusion with Senator Lodge and Captain Mahan; but, while there was certainly irresponsibility in what Roosevelt did, as in what the other American officials did, there was nothing that stands out as villainy; and Roosevelt, from an early stage, was to favor disengagement from the Philippine commitment at the first opportunity. He was, in fact, to become the advocate of a policy whereby the Far East would be left as a Japanese sphere-of-influence.

The same general point may be made about the succession of American presidents who, step by step, involved the United States far deeper in Vietnam than had been intended. (One hopes that history will ultimately give President Lyndon Johnson the credit due him for having at last reversed course on March 31, 1968, adopting the new objective of disengagement from Vietnam.)

William Butler Yeats wrote:

> They must to keep their certainty accuse
> All that are different of a base intent;
> Pull down established honour; hawk for news
> Whatever their loose phantasy invent
> And murmur it with bated breath, as though
> The abounding gutter had been Helicon
> Or calumny a song.